D0757594

Better Homes and Gardens®

Easy Menus for DINING IN

Meredith Books • Des Moines, Iowa

Better Homes and Gardens® Books
An imprint of Meredith® Books

Easy Menus for Dining In

Project Manager: Kristi M. Thomas
Contributing Editors: Karen Fraley, Gretchen Kauffman, Susan Kling,
    Spectrum Communication Services Inc.
Recipe Developers: Bev Bennet, Brett Champion, Robin Davis,
    Dotty Griffith, Jacki Newgent
Writers: David Feder, Marge Perry
Graphic Designers: Studio P2 (Craig Hanken, Bethanie Aswegan)
Copy Chief: Terri Fredrickson
Copy and Production Editor: Victoria Forlini
Editorial Operations Manager: Karen Schirm
Managers, Book Production: Pam Kvitne, Marjorie J. Schenkelberg,
    Rick von Holdt
Photographers: Marty Baldwin, Jay Wilde
Food Stylist: Charles Worthington
Prop Stylist: Karen Johnson
Indexer: Martha Fifield
Electronic Production Coordinator: Paula Forest
Editorial and Design Assistants: Karen McFadden, Mary Lee Gavin
Test Kitchen Director: Lynn Blanchard
Test Kitchen Product Supervisor: Colleen Weeden

Meredith® Books

Editor in Chief: Linda Raglan Cunningham
Design Director: Matt Strelecki
Executive Editor, Food and Crafts: Jennifer Dorland Darling

Publisher: James D. Blume
Executive Director, Marketing: Jeffrey Myers
Executive Director, New Business Development: Todd M. Davis
Executive Director, Sales: Ken Zagor
Director, Operations: George A. Susral
Director, Production: Douglas M. Johnston
Business Director: Jim Leonard

Vice President and General Manager: Douglas J. Guendel

Better Homes and Gardens® Magazine

Editor in Chief: Karol DeWulf Nickell
Deputy Editor, Food and Entertaining: Nancy Hopkins
Meredith Publishing Group
President, Publishing Group: Stephen M. Lacy
Vice President-Publishing Director: Bob Mate

Meredith Corporation

Chairman and Chief Executive Officer: William T. Kerr

In Memoriam: E. T. Meredith III (1933-2003)

All of us at Better Homes and Gardens® Books are dedicated to providing you with the information and ideas you need to create delicious foods. We welcome your comments and suggestions. Write to us at: Better Homes and Gardens Books, Cookbook Editorial Department, 1716 Locust St., Des Moines, IA 50309-3023.

If you would like to purchase any of our cooking, crafts, gardening, home improvement, or home decorating and design books, check wherever quality books are sold. Or visit us at: bhgbooks.com

Our seal assures you that every recipe in *Easy Menus for Dining In* has been tested in the Better Homes and Gardens® Test Kitchen. This means that each recipe is practical and reliable, and meets our high standards of taste appeal. We guarantee your satisfaction with this book for as long as you own it.

Copyright © 2003 by Meredith Corporation,
Des Moines, Iowa. First Edition.
All rights reserved. Printed in the
United States of America.
Library of Congress Control Number:
2003104117
ISBN: 0-696-21715-5

Photo: Berry Clafouti, page 253

Table of Contents

Home Dining—In Style

The art of dining at home is more than just sitting down to a hot meal with your sanity intact. Although planning, shopping, and preparation for a special meal might seem daunting, it doesn't have to. The trick is to plan ahead and map out the steps. A picture-perfect, gastronomically exquisite meal, akin to one at your favorite restaurant, can be achieved.

With *Easy Menus for Dining In,* the hardest part has been eliminated: what to have and how to plan your time. Here you'll find time organizers and 16 doable menus—including appetizers, entrées, sides, and desserts. Options are built in, so if something doesn't pique your interest, you have other appetizer, entrée, or dessert recipes to choose from.

You'll also learn practical ways to set up a kitchen and shop for ingredients. Ideas for making your meal more special are also included with each menu. Your efforts will yield big dividends when your family and friends form lasting memories of enjoying home-cooked meals together.

So get ready to be inspired for some very fine meals to relish at home.

Kitchen Basics

The aspiring kitchen wizard has some great advantages already at hand. The most important of those are the true love of cooking, eating, and creating memorable dishes. You can learn to be a crackerjack in the kitchen. Be assured, the only difference between being able to prepare one recipe well and 1,000 recipes well is practice. To think and create like a great cook, you don't need to conquer difficult or fussy recipes, and you don't need a retinue of helpers (unless, of course, you love company while in the kitchen). Great meals depend on knowing a few simple concepts and mastering some basics. The following suggestions will help you become a great cook at home.

Follow Your Nose

When choosing fruits and vegetables, use all of your senses. Due to extensive crossbreeding on factory farms, good-looking produce is often the norm rather than the exception.

Use your eyes, of course, to spot bruises or tears, but don't stop there. Pick up each item with deliberation. Feel the weight of it in your hand. The best produce feels heavier than it looks.

Now smell it. Most fruits and vegetables will give off the fresh aroma of their flesh when ripe. The scent of truly fresh and succulent produce, such as mangoes, apples, sweet corn, or leafy greens, will transport you to another realm—a Caribbean island, a New England orchard, the rich earth of a Midwestern cornfield, or a West Coast field of greens.

Sound can play a part too. The muted thump (versus hollow echo) of a juice-heavy melon or the rustling crackle of fresh green chard will confirm freshness. And your sense of touch—from the delicate firmness of a portobello mushroom to the taut skin of the fuzzy kiwifruit to the deceptively slight give of a perfect avocado—gives you more clues.

Only the Best Is Best

Always use the best ingredients available. In cooking, sparing no expense on the ingredients is not indulgent or lavish; rather, it is the basis for great-tasting finished dishes. In all cases, the difference between fresh and processed is monumental. Herbs are a good example.

Use fresh whenever you can. Dried herbs are convenient to use, however. Buy them in small amounts and store them, well-sealed, in a cool, dry place. The same holds true for spices. Buy spices in their whole forms whenever possible and use a mortar and pestle or grinder (an electric grinder or one similar to your pepper grinder) to grind them on an as-needed basis. When you use ground spices, make sure they are fresh. If you store your spice products properly, here's a guideline of how long they may last.

Storing Dried Herbs and Spices

Store dried herbs and spices in airtight containers in a dry place away from sunlight and heat. Replace them when their aroma fades. Generally, whole spices and herbs keep 1 to 2 years (whole cloves, nutmeg, and cinnamon sticks will maintain their quality slightly beyond 2 years). Ground herbs and spices maintain their quality up to 6 months. Refrigerate red spices, such as paprika and chili powder, to preserve their flavor and color.

Top-Notch Equipment

You'll be surprised how little you need in the way of equipment in order to prepare stunning meals. At home, you can do better than 90 percent of your cooking using nothing more than a chef's knife or French knife with an 8- to 14-inch blade, a cutting board, a couple of skillets, a large and a small saucepan, and a pair of tongs. Equipment is an example

of getting what you pay for, so consider carefully what you need before you buy. A set of high-quality pots, pans, and utensils, for example, can set you back almost as much as the appliances in your kitchen.

A good guideline to follow is to spend what you can afford for a lifetime of service. A $90 saucepan that will last for several decades ends up costing far less than the $10 saucepan you have to toss after a year or two. Quality pots and pans are heavy, have thick walls and bottoms (which allow for even heat distribution), and have sturdy handles that will dissipate heat.

A good knife—with forged high-carbon steel and stain-resistant blades—is absolutely imperative in the kitchen. It will be thick and rigid and have considerable weight, yet feel balanced in your hand. Good knives hold their edge; this is important because a dull knife can be more dangerous than a sharp one. Dull knives have to be forced into doing the job, which means greater risk for slippage.

One inexpensive purchase you should consider is a good pair of tongs. Sturdy 8-inch-long metal tongs with a strong spring are extensions of the professional chef's hands. Extremely hot temperatures limit where even quick fingers dare to go. Use tongs for grabbing, turning, stirring, and plucking foods with ease.

Additionally, you'd be hard pressed to find a tool as versatile as a vegetable peeler. Keep several stashed throughout the kitchen, not only for paring but also for making ribbons of firm vegetables, such as carrots, celery root, or summer squash. A peeler also can be used to zest citrus fruits or to shave the flat side of a chocolate square for beautiful curls to garnish a dessert.

Read Before You Leap

Creativity in the kitchen requires experimentation, but when making a recipe for the first time, follow it to the letter. In fact, read it through several times. Prepare it in your head. Divide the steps into smaller steps. Check off all of the ingredients. When you are ready to prepare the recipe, set the ingredients out in the order in which you'll use them. If the recipe says to preheat the oven, do exactly that. If it calls for butter rather than margarine, use butter. This extra effort and attention to details will ensure success with your creations.

Pantry Basics

There are certain ingredients you should always have on hand. For the pantry, keep a bottle each of quality olive oil for quick sautes or dressings, and pure cooking oil, such as canola, grapeseed, peanut, safflower, or soybean. These are better for frying because they have a higher smoking point; they do not break down as easily, which will give your food an unpleasant flavor. A small bottle of good balsamic vinegar will stand ready for adding quick splashes of flavor to sauces, dressings, and even fruit salads.

A twist of coarse sea salt from a hand mill (such as is used for pepper) is one of the easiest ways to brighten savory dishes. Sea salt has more power and depth of flavor than regular table salt (see "salt" in Glossary, page 17). Sea salt has additional trace minerals that round out the sodium, letting a little go a long way. Grind black pepper as you go too. Whole peppercorns retain more of the sweet and less of the heat because the volatile oils that give pepper its flavor stay trapped until you release them with a turn of the wrist.

Have fresh garlic on hand. The flavor of fresh garlic is light years ahead of dried and of refrigerated minced garlic. Also, nothing gives a recipe that "processed" taste more than powdered garlic.

For adding shots of flavor, keep plenty of condiments such as the following on hand: high-quality mustards, hot pepper sauce, relishes, seasoning blends, olives, capers, prepared horseradish, soy sauce, chutneys, Worcestershire sauce. You'll be surprised at how much just a dash of bottled hot pepper sauce will spark the flavors in stews, soups, and pasta sauces.

Pretty as a Picture

Garnishes often daunt home chefs who perceive that an elaborate embellishment is a mandatory part of executing the perfect plate. Nothing could be farther from the truth. Sometimes a plate needs nothing more than a little twist, a different arrangement that results in an "a-ha!" presentation. This comes from using the ingredients to their best—and most attractive—advantage.

For example, just two long, slender chives crossed delicately over the food or a sprinkling of fresh herbs chiffonade-style (see Glossary, page 16) can be quietly impressive. A fresh herb-and-oil blend drizzled over a piece of salmon on a stark white plate offers stunning results. Keep small strainers on hand to dust desserts and plates with cocoa or powdered sugar, which will give once ho-hum desserts a whole new sophistication.

Look at foods or ingredients in new or different ways. For example, cut an avocado crosswise to create rings, then stack them to make a cup for a relish. This is both surprising and comforting: surprising that something so basic can be made to look extraordinary; comforting in that it is simple enough for anyone to re-create.

Wine

When you go to a good restaurant, you expect to be served a good wine. You should treat yourself in the same manner in your own home. Fortunately, you can be more adventurous at home because you're not limited to a wine list. Also, because restaurants mark up wines considerably, you can usually get the same wine at the liquor store for a better price. It is important to note that a high price tag doesn't always mean the wine is of high quality. Supply-and-demand often determines cost. If you're really unsure, seek out a good wine shop and ask questions. Most likely a staff person can help you sift through the labels and types of wine to determine the best one for your special dinner. There are also helpful books on the market (one to look for is Kevin Zraly's *Complete Wine Course,* Sterling Publishing Co., Inc., 2000). The more basic the book, the better. Or check the Internet for sites such as winetoday.com or winespectator.com for tips.

Serving Tips

Wine Temperature

If a white wine is served too cold, the true character, flavor, and aroma will be diminished. If a red wine is served too warm, it will change the balance of the flavor components and hamper the taste of the wine. The rule about serving red wine at room temperature doesn't apply because most rooms today are kept warmer than in the past. It's best if red wine is chilled ever so briefly (10 minutes in an ice bucket or a half hour in the refrigerator) to bring it to the correct temperature. Here are a few temperature guidelines.

- **High-quality Chardonnays** are best served at 55°F to 60°F. White wines made from **Sauvignon Blanc** or **Riesling** are best served at 45°F to 55°F.
- **Champagnes and sparkling wines** taste best when served at 45°F.
- **Lighter reds** (Beaujolais, Pinot Noir) are better served at 55°F to 60°F, while **Cabernet Sauvignon** and **Merlot** taste best at 60°F to 65°F.
- **Sauternes** should be served from 58°F to 62°F. **Ports** are best between 62°F and 65°F.

Wine Storage Temperatures

Wine will age more quickly if stored at warm temperatures (70°F or so). Fluctuations in temperature are not good for wine either. Therefore, it is best to store both red and white wines in the refrigerator, where you know it won't get warm or experience wild fluctuations in temperature. (Of course, if you have a wine cellar, you should store your wine there.)

Wine Glasses

The classic rules about using the appropriate glass with various wines have merit. A smaller glass that becomes narrower at the top helps keep a white wine chilled and concentrates the bouquet. A larger, bulbous-shape glass is appropriate for red wines because it allows the wine to have more contact with air, which helps the flavor develop. The narrow, fluted glass for champagne or sparkling wine keeps the bubbles intact and preserves the fizz. It also helps concentrate the bouquet.

Cabernets and **Merlots** are often denser and richer wines than Pinot Noirs and don't require a balloon-shaped glass.

The smaller size of the **white wine** glass helps keep the wine chilled. A larger surface area would cause the wine to warm to room temperature too quickly.

The narrow, fluted glass for **Champagne** or **sparkling wine** keeps the bubbles intact and preserves the fizz.

The **port** glass is smaller than other wine glasses to accommodate a smaller serving. Due to the intense flavor of port, it doesn't require much room for the flavor and aroma to build.

The **Pinot Noir** glass is large with a bulbous shape, to allow more flavor and aroma development for this characteristically delicate and refined wine.

Wine and Food Compatibility

There are no steadfast rules when it comes to pairing wine and food. But some foods just taste better with certain wines. Generally, however, the fuller the food's flavor, the fuller-flavored and fuller-bodied (which refers to the wine feeling heavy or light on your tongue) the wine ought to be. Here is just a short list of wines and foods that are compatible. Note that wines can cross over between categories of light- or full-bodied depending on the winery or region they come from.

Red Wines

	Beaujolais	Cabernet	Merlot	Pinot Noir	Port	Zinfandel
Appetizers	O	—	—	—	—	—
Asian food	—	—	—	—	—	—
Beef	—	O	O	O	—	O
Cheese (mild)	—	—	—	—	—	—
Cheese (strong)	O	O	O	O	O	O
Chocolate	—	O	O	—	O	—
Fruit/Dessert	—	—	—	—	—	—
Pasta w/cream sauce	—	—	—	—	—	—
Pasta w/red sauce	O	O	O	O	—	O
Pork	O	—	—	O	—	—
Poultry	O	—	—	—	—	—
Seafood	—	—	—	—	—	—

Source: wine.about.com

White Wines

	Chardonnay	Chenin Blanc	Dry Reisling	Gewürz-traminer	Sauv. Blanc	White Reisling
Appetizers	O	O	O	O	O	—
Asian food	—	O	O	O	—	—
Beef	—	—	—	—	—	—
Cheese (mild)	—	O	O	O	O	O
Cheese (strong)	O	O	O	—	O	—
Chocolate	—	—	—	—	—	O
Grilled Fish	O	—	O	—	O	—
Oysters	O	—	—	—	O	—
Pasta w/cream sauce	—	—	—	—	O	—
Pasta w/red sauce	—	—	—	—	—	—
Pork	O	—	O	O	—	—
Poultry	O	O	O	O	O	—
Seafood w/light sauce	O	—	O	—	O	—
Seafood w/cream sauce	O	—	—	—	—	—
Shellfish	—	O	—	—	O	—
Shrimp, crab, lobster	—	O	O	—	O	—

Source: wine.about.com

Glossary

Do you feel a little lost when reading food terms or ingredients used in cookbooks? Here is a list of culinary terms and foods to help you know what's what.

baste: To brush a food item, such as a roast, with its own juices or a liquid while it cooks.

bouquet garni: A bundle of herbs, such as parsley, bay, and thyme, used for flavoring stocks, soups, or stews.

caramelize: Caramelized sugar is cooked and stirred in a dry pan until it is brown and liquid. Caramelized onions or leeks are cooked, with little stirring, in a skillet until their natural sugars turn the vegetables brown.

chiffonade (shihf-uh-NAHD): A French word meaning "made of rags." It means to cut food (such as lettuce, sorrel, or herbs) into thin ribbons using a sharp knife; to shred.

cube: To cut into ½-inch cubes.

demi-glace (DEHM-ee glahs): Meaning "half glaze" in French, this refers to a stock that has been thickened through reduction (see "reduce"). It is usually used to make other sauces. To purchase, look for it at your supermarket or check morethangourmet.com.

dice: To cut into ¼-inch cubes.

emulsion: A stable combination of two generally unmixable ingredients, such as oil and vinegar. Mayonnaise is an example of an emulsion.

fines herbes (FEENZ ehrb): Finely chopped mixture of four herbs, usually chervil, parsley, tarragon, and marjoram or thyme.

fold: To gently combine an airy mixture, such as beaten egg whites, into a thicker mixture, such as cake batter, without breaking down the lighter mixture. To fold, use a rubber spatula to cut down and through the mixture, moving across the bottom of the bowl and coming back up, folding some of the mixture from the bottom over the top.

gratin: A topping of either cheese or a mixture of butter and bread crumbs that is broiled or heated until brown. Special shallow dishes, called gratin dishes, have a larger surface area, allowing for a greater portion of topping per serving.

infusion: Flavor extraction derived from steeping an herb, spice, or tea in a liquid.

julienne: To cut into thin, small strips generally the size and shape of matchsticks. Although the dimensions are not standard, what matters is that all of the strips are about the same size so that they cook evenly.

mandoline: A hand-operated utensil with adjustable blades used for shredding and slicing, including decorative slices such as waffle cuts.

measuring cup, dry: Cups that have no spouts. For an accurate measure, spoon ingredient into cup and level off with the flat side of a knife. (Do not shake!)

measuring cup, liquid: Glass or clear plastic measuring cups, with spouts, for measuring liquids. For an accurate measure, bend down so your eye is level with the markings on the cup.

mince: To cut or chop food into very small, somewhat even pieces. Minced food is smaller in size than finely chopped food.

mirepoix (mihr-PWAH): A mixture of chopped carrot, onion, and celery used to flavor stocks, soups, stews, or other dishes. It is generally comprised of 50 percent onions, 25 percent carrots, and 25 percent celery.

poivre (PWAHV-r): French for "pepper"; steak au poivre is a steak heavily coated in coarsely ground or whole peppercorns before cooking.

prosciutto: Italian ham that has been salted and air-cured rather than smoked.

puree: To change a solid food into a liquid or heavy paste, usually by using a blender, food processor, or food mill; also refers to the resulting mixture.

reduce: To boil a liquid rapidly until the volume reduces through evaporation, which thickens or intensifies the flavor of the liquid. This reduction, as it is called, often is a broth, stock, wine, or sauce. Using the correct pan size for this process is critical. If you use a pan that is too small, the liquid will not have enough surface area and will take a longer time to evaporate.

rice noodles, rice sticks, rice vermicelli: Noodles, thin "sticks," or vermicelli made from rice flour.

roulade (roo-LAHD): A French term for a thin slice of meat or poultry that is spread with a filling, rolled up, and secured with a toothpick or kitchen string. It is usually browned before baking or braising.

roux (ROO): A French term that refers to a mixture of flour and fat cooked to a golden or rich brown color. It is used as a thickener for sauces, soups, and stews.

salt, Fleur de Sel de Guerande: From Brittany, on the coast of France, this salt is harvested from the surface of the sea by hand and is considered the crème de la crème of salts. French chefs suggest using this salt as a condiment, such as a sprinkling it lightly over a swipe of sweet butter on country French bread.

salt, kosher: Less salty, measure for measure, than table salt, kosher salt is an additive-free, coarse-flaked salt. It is often used in preparation of kosher meats.

salt, sea: Evaporated from sea water, sea salt contains higher mineral content than table salt, which gives it a distinctive flavor.

salt, table: A fine-grained salt with additives that create a free-flowing product.

saute: To cook something in a small amount of oil over high heat; from the French word for "jump."

simmer: To cook food gently (below the boiling point) where small bubbles just break the surface.

snip: To use kitchen shears to finely cut up foods, such as fresh herbs or dried fruit.

vanilla bean paste: A syruplike product that contains finely ground vanilla bean seeds. To buy vanilla paste, check King Arthur Flour's catalog or web site (kingarthurflour.com) or Williams Sonoma's catalog or web site (williams-sonoma.com).

wasabi (WAH-sah-bee): A Japanese condiment that comes from the root of the wasabi plant, usually served mashed into a paste. Wasabi's light green color belies its heat. Also called Japanese horseradish, it is often served with sushi or sashimi.

whisk: A kitchen utensil made from wire loops attached to a handle, it is used for beating ingredients lightly and rapidly to incorporate air.

zest: The colored outer skin of citrus fruits used to add flavor to foods. Remove the zest with a fruit zester, small-holed grater, paring knife, or vegetable peeler. Avoid using the white membrane beneath the peel, which is bitter.

Equivalents

When a recipe calls for a measurement of food or fresh produce and you don't know how much to buy, use these guidelines to help determine what you will need.

Food	Beginning size or amount	Yield and cut
Apple	1 medium	1 cup sliced or ²/₃ cup chopped
Apricots	1 pound (8 to 12 whole)	2¹/₂ cups sliced
Asparagus	1 pound (18 to 24 spears)	2 to 2¹/₂ cups 1-inch pieces
Banana	1 medium	¹/₃ cup mashed or ³/₄ cup sliced
Beans, green	1 pound	3 to 3¹/₂ cups 1-inch pieces
Blueberries	1 pound	3 cups
Broccoli	1 pound	4 cups florets
Cabbage	1 medium head (1¹/₂ pounds)	7 to 10 cups shredded or 6 cups coarsely chopped
Carrot	1 medium	¹/₂ cup sliced, chopped, julienned, or finely shredded
Cauliflower	1 medium head (1¹/₂ pounds)	6 cups florets
Celery	1 stalk	¹/₂ cup sliced or chopped
Cherries	1 pound	3 cups whole or 2¹/₂ cups halved
Chocolate chips	6 ounces	1 cup
Cranberries	1 pound	4 cups
Cream, whipping	1 cup unwhipped	2 cups whipped
Garlic	1 clove	¹/₂ teaspoon minced
Grapes	1 pound	2¹/₂ cups
Leek	1 medium	¹/₃ cup sliced
Lemon	1 medium	2 teaspoons finely shredded peel 3 tablespoons juice
Lime	1 medium	1¹/₂ teaspoons finely shredded peel 2 tablespoons juice
Mango	1 medium	1 cup sliced
Melon		
Cantaloupe	1 medium (2¹/₂ pounds)	6 cups cubed or 5¹/₂ cups balls
Honeydew	1 medium (2¹/₂ pounds)	6 cups cubed or 5¹/₂ cups balls
Mushrooms	8 ounces	3 cups sliced or chopped
Nectarine	1 medium	1 cup sliced or ³/₄ cup chopped
Onion	1 medium	¹/₂ cup chopped
Onion, green	1 medium	2 tablespoons sliced
Orange	1 medium	1 tablespoon finely shredded peel ¹/₃ cup juice or ¹/₃ cup sections
Papaya	1 medium (1 pound)	1¹/₄ cups sliced
Parsnip	1 medium	³/₄ to 1 cup sliced or chopped
Peach	1 medium	1 cup sliced or ³/₄ cup chopped
Pear	1 medium	1 cup sliced or chopped
Pepper, sweet	1 medium	1 cup strips or ³/₄ cup chopped
Potatoes	1 pound	3 cups cubed (unpeeled) or 2³/₄ cups cubed (peeled)
Pineapple	1 medium (4 pounds)	4¹/₂ cups peeled and cubed
Raspberries	1 pound	4 cups
Rice, long grain	1 cup uncooked	3 cups cooked
Rhubarb	1 pound	4 cups sliced
Shallot	1 medium	2 tablespoons finely chopped
Squash		
Summer (zucchini, yellow)	1 medium	1¹/₄ cups sliced
Winter (acorn, butternut)	2 pounds	4 cups chopped or 2 cups mashed
Strawberries	1 pint (about 1 pound)	3 cups whole or 2¹/₂ cups sliced
Tomato	1 medium	¹/₂ cup peeled, seeded, and chopped

Emergency Substitutions

Running low on an ingredient can put you in a bind when you're in a hurry and have no time to go to the store. This list of substitutions will come to the rescue.

It you don't have:	Substitute:
Baking powder, 1 teaspoon	½ teaspoon cream of tartar plus ¼ teaspoon baking soda
Balsamic vinegar, 1 tablespoon	1 tablespoon cider vinegar or red wine vinegar plus ½ teaspoon sugar
Bread crumbs, fine dry, ¼ cup	¾ cup soft bread crumbs, or ¼ cup cracker crumbs, or ¼ cup cornflake crumbs
Broth, beef or chicken, 1 cup	1 teaspoon or 1 cube instant beef or chicken bouillon plus 1 cup hot water
Buttermilk, 1 cup	1 tablespoon lemon juice or vinegar plus enough milk to make 1 cup (let stand 5 minutes before using), or 1 cup plain yogurt
Chocolate, semisweet, 1 ounce	3 tablespoons semisweet chocolate pieces, or 1 ounce unsweetened chocolate plus 1 tablespoon granulated sugar, or 1 tablespoon unsweetened cocoa powder plus 2 teaspoons sugar and 2 teaspoons shortening
Chocolate, sweet baking, 4 ounces	¼ cup unsweetened cocoa powder plus ⅓ cup granulated sugar and 3 tablespoons shortening
Chocolate, unsweetened, 1 ounce	3 tablespoons unsweetened cocoa powder plus 1 tablespoon cooking oil or melted shortening
Cornstarch, 1 tablespoon (for thickening)	2 tablespoons all-purpose flour
Corn syrup (light), 1 cup	1 cup granulated sugar plus ¼ cup water
Egg, 1 whole	2 egg whites, or 2 egg yolks, or ¼ cup refrigerated or frozen egg product, thawed
Flour, cake, 1 cup	1 cup minus 2 tablespoons all-purpose flour
Flour, self-rising, 1 cup	1 cup all-purpose flour plus 1 teaspoon baking powder, ½ teaspoon salt, and ¼ teaspoon baking soda
Garlic, 1 clove	½ teaspoon bottled minced garlic or ⅛ teaspoon garlic powder
Ginger, grated fresh, 1 teaspoon	¼ teaspoon ground ginger
Molasses, 1 cup	1 cup honey
Mustard, dry, 1 teaspoon	1 tablespoon prepared (in cooked mixtures)
Mustard, prepared, 1 tablespoon	½ teaspoon dry mustard plus 2 teaspoons vinegar
Onion, chopped, ½ cup	2 tablespoons dried minced onion or ½ teaspoon onion powder
Sour cream, dairy, 1 cup	1 cup plain yogurt
Sugar, granulated, 1 cup	1 cup packed brown sugar or 2 cups sifted powdered sugar
Sugar, brown, 1 cup packed	1 cup granulated sugar plus 2 tablespoons molasses
Tomato juice, 1 cup	½ cup tomato sauce plus ½ cup water
Tomato sauce, 2 cups	¾ cup tomato paste plus 1 cup water
Vanilla bean, 1 whole	2 teaspoons vanilla extract
Wine, red, 1 cup	1 cup beef or chicken broth in savory recipes; cranberry juice in desserts
Wine, white, 1 cup	1 cup chicken broth in savory recipes; apple juice or white grape juice in desserts
Yeast, active dry, 1 package	about 2¼ teaspoons active dry yeast

Seasonings*

Apple pie spice, 1 teaspoon	½ teaspoon ground cinnamon plus ¼ teaspoon ground nutmeg, ⅛ teaspoon ground allspice, and dash ground cloves or ginger
Cajun seasoning, 1 tablespoon	½ teaspoon white pepper, ½ teaspoon garlic powder, ½ teaspoon onion powder, ½ teaspoon ground red pepper, ½ teaspoon paprika, and ½ teaspoon black pepper
Herbs, snipped fresh, 1 tablespoon	½ to 1 teaspoon dried herb, crushed, or ½ teaspoon ground herb
Poultry seasoning, 1 teaspoon	¾ teaspoon dried sage, crushed, plus ¼ teaspoon dried thyme or marjoram, crushed
Pumpkin pie spice, 1 teaspoon	½ teaspoon ground cinnamon plus ¼ teaspoon ground ginger, ¼ teaspoon ground allspice, and ⅛ teaspoon ground nutmeg

Exotic Endeavors

Menu

Fig and Fruit Salad, page 22

Moroccan Lamb with Couscous,
  page 24

Steamed sugar snap peas

Pita bread

Caramelized Quince Tart, page 25

Menu Options

Do you love culinary adventures? Experimenting with new ingredients and techniques, exploring the cuisines of faraway lands? This is the menu for the passionate culinary explorer.

Learn how to use new or unusual ingredients such as quince, the fruit that is a cross between and apple and a pear, and makes a lovely and unusual tart (see page 25). Try new fare such as Moroccan Lamb with Couscous, Toasted Honey-Fennel Pound Cake, and Mango and Cream Tart for new taste sensations.

Set the stage for a special meal with an orchid.

Once found only in the tropics, orchids are now available at many supermarkets, nurseries, and home centers—all of which tend to offer these long-blooming flowers less expensively than a florist. The photo shows one idea for using these exquisite flowers. Remove the orchid from its plastic container (if it has one) and surround it with stones in a glass container. Or place a single stem in a bud vase at each plate for an elegant beginning to an extraordinary dining experience.

ToDo:

Up to 24 Hours Ahead

- Prepare dressing for Fig and Fruit Salad; cover and refrigerate.
- Prepare Buttery Pastry for Caramelized Quince Tart; wrap ball of pastry in plastic wrap. Refrigerate.

1¼ Hours Ahead

- Remove Buttery Pastry from refrigerator.
- Begin preparing Lamb with Couscous.

1 Hour Ahead

- Assemble tart.
- Prepare salads; arrange on salad plates. Refrigerate until serving time.

45 Minutes Ahead

- Preheat oven for tart.

35 Minutes Ahead

- Begin baking tart.

45 Minutes Ahead

- Add dried fruit to lamb mixture.
- Cook sugar snap peas.

5 Minutes Ahead

- Turn tart out onto serving plate.
- Finish lamb.
- Toss butter with sugar snap peas.

Fig and Fruit Salad

Tender leaves of spinach and toasted walnuts—tossed with a walnut oil and rice vinegar dressing—become the backdrop for this beautiful salad. Figs, oranges, grapefruit, and goat cheese are arranged on top of the salad.

Ingredients

3 tablespoons rice vinegar

3 tablespoons walnut oil

1 small clove garlic, minced

2 tablespoons snipped fresh mint

½ teaspoon salt

⅛ teaspoon black pepper

5 cups torn fresh spinach

2 oranges and/or blood oranges,
    peeled and sliced crosswise

10 dried Calimyrna (light or golden) figs

3 ounces semisoft goat cheese (chèvre)
    rolled in cracked black pepper or
    herbs, broken into large chunks
    (optional)

⅓ cup walnuts, toasted

Start to Finish: 25 minutes **Makes:** 5 appetizer servings

1 For dressing, in a blender container or food processor bowl combine rice vinegar, walnut oil, garlic, mint, salt, and pepper. Cover and blend or process until nearly smooth.

2 In a large bowl drizzle spinach with dressing; toss gently to coat. Divide spinach mixture among 5 salad bowls or plates. Halve half of the figs lengthwise. Arrange orange slices and figs with spinach mixture. If desired, top with goat cheese. Top with walnuts.

Nutrition Facts per serving: 257 cal., 19 g total fat (5 g sat. fat), 13 mg chol., 360 mg sodium, 18 g carbo., 6 g fiber, 7 g pro.

Roasted Fruit Soup

Using a high oven temperature concentrates the mulled-fruit flavor of the pear, plums, cranberries, and apple in this gently spiced dessert.

Ingredients

1 cup fresh cranberries (4 ounces)

½ cup packed brown sugar

1 medium pear, cored and cut into
   thin wedges

1 medium cooking apple (such as
   Rome, Jonathan, or Fuji), cored
   and cut into wedges

3 plums, halved and pitted

3 cups cranberry-apple juice

1 tablespoon lemon juice

2 3-inch pieces stick cinnamon

Prep: 10 minutes   **Roast:** 35 minutes   **Oven:** 450°F
Makes: 6 appetizer servings

1 In a 3-quart rectangular baking dish stir together cranberries and brown sugar. Add pear and apple wedges. Roast, uncovered, in a 450° oven about 20 minutes or just until fruit is tender. Add plum halves. Roast, uncovered, about 15 minutes more or until fruit is tender and edges of fruit begin to brown or curl. Stir gently to combine.

2 Meanwhile, in a large saucepan combine cranberry-apple juice, lemon juice, and stick cinnamon. Bring to boiling; reduce heat. Simmer, uncovered, for 10 minutes. Remove the cinnamon sticks; discard. Gently stir roasted fruits and their juices into mixture in saucepan. Spoon roasted fruit soup into serving bowls.

Nutrition Facts per serving: 185 cal., 0 g total fat (0 g sat. fat), 0 mg chol., 7 mg sodium, 47 g carbo., 3 g fiber, 1 g pro.

Art of Asian

Menu

Mixed-Greens Salad
   with Ginger Vinaigrette, page 38

Sea Bass with Chile Oil, page 39

Coconut Rice with Snow Peas, page 40

Star Anise Rice Cream, page 41

Purchased almond cookies

Menu Options

Shiitake and Lemongrass Soup, page 42

Mandarin Apricot Chicken Wings, page 43

Sesame Beef Kabobs, page 44

Caramelized Chicken and Rice Noodles,
   page 45

Indonesian Curry, page 46

Thai-Style Shrimp Soup, page 49

Asian Braised Short Ribs, page 50

Ginger Crème Brûlée, page 51

Across the country, Asian eateries—representing the cuisines of Japan, China, Thailand, Korea, Malaysia, India, and Vietnam—have been opening up, exposing more of us to the wonderful varied cuisines. Now, many of the ingredients used in Asian foods—soy sauce, lemon grass, coconut milk, hoisin sauce, and ginger—are available in the grocery store, which means you can replicate these wonderful flavors at home. Learn to balance the piquant flavor of ginger, to incorporate coconut milk as a luscious background for rice, to use lemongrass, and more when you create this exotic menu.

Set the mood by draping your table with a

cloth featuring an Asian motif, and serve tea as the beverage. Roll plain cloth napkins and tie them with a scallion (green onion). Keep the table setting minimalistic. Top the table with an Asian teapot or use single flowers and simple arrangements of flowers to decorate the table.

ToDo:

Up to 24 Hours Ahead

- Prepare Star Anise Rice Cream through Step 1.
- Prepare vinaigrette for Mixed-Greens Salad with Ginger Vinaigrette. Cover and refrigerate.
- Thaw fish in the refrigerator, if frozen.

Up to 5 Hours Ahead

- Freeze and ripen rice cream.

35 Minutes Ahead

- Assemble ingredients and begin cooking Coconut Rice with Snow Peas.
- Arrange greens and vegetables for salad on salad plates. Refrigerate until serving time. Let vinaigrette for salad stand at room temperature.

25 Minutes Ahead

- Prepare Sea Bass with Chile Oil.

10 Minutes Ahead

- Add pea pods or asparagus to rice; cook 5 minutes more.

5 Minutes Ahead

- Let rice stand for 5 minutes.

For Dessert

- Serve rice cream with cookies.

Coconut Rice with Snow Peas

Coconut milk, with its rich coconut flavor, turns rice into a perfect side dish for Asian entrées. Look for it in the ethnic foods aisle of the supermarket.

Ingredients

¾ cup water

⅔ cup unsweetened canned coconut milk

½ cup long grain rice

¼ teaspoon salt

1½ cups 2-inch bias-sliced fresh snow peas or fresh asparagus pieces

Prep: 10 minutes **Cook:** 20 minutes
Stand: 5 minutes **Makes:** 4 side-dish servings

1 In a medium saucepan combine the water, coconut milk, uncooked rice, and salt. Bring to boiling; reduce heat. Simmer, covered, for 15 minutes.

2 Place snow peas on top of the rice. Cover; cook about 5 minutes more or until rice and vegetables are tender. Remove from heat; let stand for 5 minutes.

Nutrition Facts per serving: 174 cal., 8 g total fat (7 g sat. fat), 0 mg chol., 161 mg sodium, 23 g carbo., 1 g fiber, 3 g pro.

Star Anise Rice Cream

This star anise-infused rice "cream" recipe is a stellar ending to any Asian dinner. Rice drink, found with canned milks or specialty foods in the supermarket, creates a subtle flavor base for the star anise. Rice Dream is one brand to look for.

Ingredients

¾ cup sugar

1 teaspoon unflavored gelatin

4 cups rice drink

4 whole star anise

4 beaten egg yolks

Whole star anise (optional)

Prep: 25 minutes **Chill:** 2 to 24 hours
Freeze: per manufacturer's directions
Ripen: 4 hours **Makes:** 10 servings

1 In a large saucepan combine sugar and gelatin. Stir in rice drink and the 4 star anise. Cook and stir over medium heat until mixture almost boils and sugar dissolves. Use a slotted spoon to remove star anise. Stir ½ cup of the hot mixture into egg yolks. Add egg mixture to rice drink mixture in pan. Cook and stir for 2 minutes more. (Do not boil or mixture may curdle.) Cool. Cover and chill for at least 2 hours or up to 24 hours.

2 Freeze mixture in a 2-quart ice cream maker according to the manufacturer's directions. Ripen for 4 hours.* To serve, spoon into serving dishes. If desired, garnish with star anise.

Nutrition Facts per serving: 116 cal., 2 g total fat (1 g sat. fat), 85 mg chol., 43 mg sodium, 23 g carbo., 0 g fiber, 2 g pro.

*Note: Ripening or hardening homemade frozen desserts improves the texture and helps keep them from melting too quickly during eating.

To ripen in a traditional-style ice cream freezer, after churning, remove the lid and dasher and cover the top of the freezer can with waxed paper or foil. Plug the hole in the lid with a small piece of cloth; replace the lid. Pack the outer freezer bucket with enough ice and rock salt to cover the top of the freezer can (use 4 cups ice to 1 cup salt). Ripen about 4 hours.

When using an ice cream freezer with an insulated freezer bowl, transfer ice cream to a covered freezerproof container and ripen in your regular freezer 4 hours (or check manufacturer's recommendations).

Menu Options

Shiitake and Lemongrass Soup

Lemongrass is often used in Asian fare. As the name implies, the herb (which resembles a green onion) tastes like lemon. Look for it in Asian markets, but in a pinch, substitute 1 teaspoon finely shredded lemon peel for the 2 tablespoons lemongrass.

Ingredients

2   tablespoons butter or margarine

½   cup finely chopped onion (1 medium)

2   tablespoons finely chopped fresh
        lemongrass (2 stalks)

3   cups mushroom broth or
        vegetable broth

8   ounces fresh shiitake mushrooms,
        sliced

1   tablespoon rice vinegar

⅛   teaspoon white pepper

1   cup coarsely chopped fresh spinach

Prep: 20 minutes   **Cook:** 25 minutes   **Makes:** 4 appetizer servings

1 In a large saucepan melt 1 tablespoon of the butter over medium-high heat. Add onion and lemongrass. Cook and stir about 5 minutes or until onion and lemongrass are tender. Add the broth. Bring to boiling; reduce heat. Simmer, uncovered, for 15 minutes. Strain the broth, discarding the onion and lemongrass.

2 Meanwhile, in a large skillet melt the remaining 1 tablespoon butter over medium-high heat. Add sliced mushrooms. Cook and stir about 5 minutes or until mushrooms are light brown around the edges. Remove from heat; set aside.

3 Stir vinegar and pepper into broth. Stir in spinach. To serve, ladle into bowls. Top with cooked mushrooms.

Nutrition Facts per serving: 80 cal., 8 g total fat (4 g sat. fat), 16 mg chol., 770 mg sodium, 6 g carbo., 2 g fiber, 2 g pro.

Mandarin Apricot Chicken Wings

Five-spice powder, honey, hoisin sauce, and sweet-and-sour sauce flavor the brush-on for these tasty wings. They're perfect appetizers for an Asian-inspired meal.

Ingredients

2   pounds chicken wing drummettes

   (about 24)

⅔   cup sweet-and-sour sauce

½   cup snipped dried apricots

⅓   cup bottled hoisin sauce

¼   cup soy sauce

2   tablespoons honey

2   cloves garlic, minced

¼   teaspoon ground ginger

¼   teaspoon five-spice powder

1   tablespoon sesame

   seeds, toasted

Prep: 15 minutes   **Bake:** 25 minutes   **Oven:** 400°F   **Makes:** 24 wings

1 Line a 15×10×1-inch baking pan or a shallow roasting pan with foil. Arrange drummettes in a single layer in prepared roasting pan. Bake in a 400° oven for 20 minutes.

2 Meanwhile, in a small saucepan stir together sweet-and-sour sauce, dried apricots, hoisin sauce, soy sauce, honey, garlic, ginger, and five-spice powder. Bring to boiling; reduce heat. Simmer, uncovered, for 5 minutes. Remove from heat.

3 Brush about ¼ cup of the sauce mixture over drummettes. Sprinkle with sesame seeds. Bake about 5 minutes more or until drummettes are no longer pink in the center. Reheat any remaining sauce until bubbly; serve with drummettes.

Nutrition Facts per wing: 86 cal., 5 g total fat (1 g sat. fat), 29 mg chol., 274 mg sodium, 7 g carbo., 0 g fiber, 5 g pro.

Sesame Beef Kabobs

A classic marinade of soy sauce, toasted sesame oil, garlic, and dry sherry is used to flavor the meat for these kabobs. Flecks of crushed red pepper add a little heat.

Ingredients

12 ounces beef flank steak

2 tablespoons soy sauce

2 tablespoons toasted sesame oil

1 green onion, sliced

2 cloves garlic, minced

1½ teaspoons sugar

1½ teaspoons dry sherry (optional)

½ teaspoon sesame seeds

½ teaspoon crushed red pepper

2 ounces fresh pea pods, trimmed
    and halved diagonally crosswise
    (about ¾ cup)

15 cherry tomatoes, halved

Prep: 30 minutes   **Marinate:** 4 to 24 hours
Grill: 17 minutes   **Makes:** 30 appetizers

1 Score both sides of meat in a diamond pattern by making shallow cuts at 1-inch intervals. Place meat in a resealable plastic bag set in a shallow dish.

2 For marinade, combine the soy sauce, toasted sesame oil, green onion, garlic, sugar, sherry (if using), sesame seeds, and crushed red pepper. Pour over meat; seal bag. Marinate in the refrigerator for at least 4 hours or up to 24 hours, turning bag occasionally.

3 Drain steak, discarding marinade. Place steak on the rack of an uncovered grill directly over medium coals. Grill for 17 to 21 minutes or to medium doneness (160°F), turning once.

4 Meanwhile, in a covered small saucepan cook pea pods in a small amount of boiling water for 2 to 4 minutes or until crisp-tender; drain.

5 To serve, cut steak into ¾-inch pieces. Place steak pieces and pea pods on wooden picks with cherry tomato halves.

Nutrition Facts per appetizer: 23 cal., 1 g total fat (0 g sat. fat), 5 mg chol., 30 mg sodium, 1 g carbo., 0 g fiber, 2 g pro.

Caramelized Chicken and Rice Noodles

If you can't find rice noodles at the supermarket, fettuccine is a good substitute. The delicate rice noodles (made from rice flour) soak up the sauce nicely.

Ingredients

6 ounces rice noodles*

¼ cup water

2 tablespoons brown sugar

2 tablespoons soy sauce

1 tablespoon cooking oil

1 medium onion, sliced

4 cloves garlic, minced

4 skinless, boneless chicken breast halves or 6 skinless, boneless chicken thighs (about 1 pound total), cut into bite-size pieces

2 medium carrots, cut into thin, bite-size strips (1 cup)

¼ teaspoon crushed red pepper

4 green onions, cut into 1-inch pieces

⅓ cup dry-roasted peanuts

Prep: 20 minutes **Stand:** 30 minutes
Cook: 11 minutes **Makes:** 4 main-dish servings

1 Break rice noodles into 3-inch pieces. In a medium bowl soak rice noodles in enough warm water to cover about 30 minutes or until tender. Drain well. Set aside.

2 Meanwhile, for sauce, in a small saucepan combine the ¼ cup water, brown sugar, and soy sauce. Bring to boiling, stirring until brown sugar dissolves. Remove sauce from heat; set aside.

3 Pour oil into a wok or large skillet. Preheat over medium-high heat. Add the onion slices; stir-fry for 3 minutes. Add garlic; stir-fry for 1 minute more. Add the chicken, carrots, and crushed red pepper and stir-fry for 2 minutes. Add sauce to wok. Cook about 4 minutes more or until the chicken is tender and no longer pink and the sauce is slightly thickened, stirring occasionally. Add soaked rice noodles and green onions to wok; stir-fry for 1 minute more or until heated through.

4 To serve, divide chicken mixture among 4 dinner plates. Sprinkle with peanuts.

*Note: Do not use thin rice noodles.

Nutrition Facts per serving: 432 cal., 12 g total fat (2 g sat. fat), 66 mg chol., 705 mg sodium, 50 g carbo., 2 g fiber, 32 g pro.

Indonesian Curry

The secret to this chicken stew is the wonderful mix of ingredients.

Ingredients

1 tablespoon grated fresh ginger

1 teaspoon ground turmeric

1 teaspoon salt

1 teaspoon sugar

1 3½- to 4-pound broiler-fryer

   chicken, cut up

4 teaspoons cooking oil

2 medium onions, cut into thin wedges

1 bay leaf

2 medium onions, cut into chunks

2 large cloves garlic

2 teaspoons Madras curry powder

1½ teaspoons ground coriander

½ teaspoon ground cinnamon

½ teaspoon cayenne pepper

1 14-ounce can unsweetened

   coconut milk

1½ kaffir lime leaves* or 1 teaspoon

   grated lime peel

Hot cooked rice (optional)

Snipped fresh cilantro

Prep: 15 minutes **Chill:** 1 to 24 hours
Cook: 45 minutes **Makes:** 5 main-dish servings

1 In a large self-sealing plastic bag combine ginger, turmeric, salt, and sugar; add chicken and toss to coat. Set in bowl; chill for at least 1 hour or up to 24 hours.

2 In a deep 12-inch skillet heat 2 teaspoons of the oil over medium-high heat. Add onion wedges and bay leaf; cook about 8 minutes or until brown. Use a slotted spoon to transfer to a plate; set aside.

3 Meanwhile, for curry paste, in a blender container combine uncooked onion chunks, garlic, curry powder, coriander, cinnamon, cayenne pepper, and 2 tablespoons water. Blend until mixture is smooth, scraping side of container with rubber spatula as necessary.

4 In the skillet heat remaining 2 teaspoons oil over medium-high heat. Add curry paste; cook for 4 to 5 minutes or until thickened, stirring occasionally. Add chicken; coat with curry paste. Simmer, covered, for 10 minutes. Stir in coconut milk, reserved onions, and lime leaves. Simmer, uncovered, about 20 minutes more or until chicken is tender and no longer pink (170°F for breast piece, 180°F for thighs and drumsticks). Remove bay leaf. To serve, if desired, serve chicken and sauce over rice. Sprinkle with snipped cilantro.

Nutrition Facts per serving: 745 cal., 55 g total fat (25 g sat. fat), 174 mg chol., 643 mg sodium, 17 g carbo., 2 g fiber, 46 g pro.

*Note: Look for kaffir lime leaves in Asian specialty stores.

Thai-Style Shrimp Soup

Coconut milk is predominant in this Thai soup. It gives the soup richness, body, and a wonderful flavor.

Ingredients

12 ounces fresh or frozen small shrimp

1 14-ounce can chicken broth

1 small zucchini, cut into thin, bite-size

    pieces (1½ cups)

1 green onion, bias-cut into 1¼-inch

    pieces

2 tablespoons minced fresh ginger

2 tablespoons minced fresh

    lemongrass (2 stalks) or

    1½ teaspoons finely shredded

    lemon peel

¼ teaspoon crushed red pepper

1 14-ounce can unsweetened

    coconut milk

2 tablespoons shredded fresh basil

2 tablespoons shaved coconut, toasted

    Fresh basil sprigs with blossoms

    (optional)

Start to Finish: 25 minutes **Makes:** 4 appetizer servings

1 Thaw shrimp, if frozen. Peel and devein shrimp. Rinse shrimp; pat dry with paper towels. Set aside.

2 In a saucepan bring broth to boiling. Add zucchini, green onion, ginger, lemongrass, and crushed red pepper. Return to boiling; reduce heat. Simmer, uncovered, for 3 minutes, stirring occasionally.

3 Add shrimp. Simmer, uncovered, for 1 to 3 minutes or until shrimp turn opaque. Stir in coconut milk. Heat through. Do not boil.

4 To serve, ladle into bowls. Top with shredded basil, coconut, and, if desired, basil sprigs.

Nutrition Facts per serving: 377 cal., 28 g total fat (24 g sat. fat), 129 mg chol., 714 mg sodium, 10 g carbo., 1 g fiber, 22 g pro.

Grilled to Perfection

G is healthful, easy—and the cleanup is a snap! Best of all, grilled food varies your menu options. Learn to create exciting flavors and to grill meats, poultry, and vegetables to perfection. Choose from steaks, chicken, shrimp, or salmon—plus grilled desserts!

For a stylish outdoor party, use garden stakes as place cards: first, paint wooden stakes desired color. Write each guest's name along the length of the stake and place it in a drinking glass. Accompany the stake with a single flower. You can also purchase individual flower tubes from the florist so that guests can take their flowers home.

ToDo:

Up to 48 Hours Ahead

- Prepare and refrigerate Herbed Oil for Grilled Endive with Prosciutto.

Up to 1½ Hours Ahead

- Prepared endive through Step 1. Cover and refrigerate until ready to grill.
- Prepare sage brush for Sage-Brushed Cowboy Steak.

1 Hour Ahead

- Prepare grill for indirect grilling and light coals, if using charcoal.
- Assemble Herb-Grilled Tomatoes through Step 1; set aside.
- Brush pears for Grilled Pears with Hazelnuts with lemon juice mixture and sprinkle with sugar. Cover and refrigerate until time for dessert.

40 Minutes Ahead

- Grill endive.
- Complete Step 1 for steak.
- Arrange sweet peppers and green onions for endive on salad plates; refrigerate until serving time.
- Grill steak (Steps 2 and 3) using indirect method.
- Let Herbed Oil stand at room temperature.

15 Minutes Ahead

- Remove endive; keep warm.
- Grill tomatoes.
- Assemble endive; drizzle with Herbed Oil.
- Complete Step 4 for steak.

For Dessert

- Replenish coals and arrange for direct grilling. Grill and serve pears.

Menu

Grilled Endive with Prosciutto

Herbed oils are popular in restaurants because they add pizzazz to the plate. If you put the oil in a clean squeeze bottle (the cheap catsup- or mustard-type you can find at the grocery store with kitchenware items), it's a breeze to drizzle the oil over the plate and food. The oil dresses up this appetizer but serves as a dressing as well.

Ingredients

1 tablespoon olive oil

1 tablespoon Dijon-style mustard

¼ teaspoon black pepper

2 heads Belgian endive, trimmed

and halved lengthwise

4 thin slices prosciutto

(1½ to 2 ounces)

½ of a medium red sweet pepper,

cut into thin strips

½ of a medium yellow sweet pepper,

cut into thin strips

1 green onion, bias-sliced

1 recipe Herbed Oil

Prep: 15 minutes **Grill:** 25 minutes **Makes:** 4 appetizer servings

1 In a small bowl combine the olive oil, mustard, and black pepper; brush over endive halves. Wrap each endive half in a thin slice of prosciutto; secure with wooden toothpicks.

2 Arrange medium-hot coals around a drip pan. Test for medium heat above the pan. Place endive on grill rack over drip pan. Cover; grill about 25 minutes or until endive is tender and prosciutto is golden brown, turning once halfway through grilling.

3 Meanwhile, in a small bowl combine the sweet peppers and green onion; divide among 4 salad plates. Top with grilled endive. Drizzle each serving and plate with Herbed Oil. Discard any remaining oil. Serve immediately.

Herbed Oil: In a blender container combine ¼ cup olive oil, ⅓ cup coarsely chopped fresh flat-leaf parsley, 3 tablespoons snipped fresh chives, 4 teaspoons snipped fresh lemon thyme or thyme, and ¼ teaspoon salt. Cover and blend until smooth. Strain herb mixture through a fine-mesh sieve, pressing on solids to extract all oil; discard herb mixture. Place oil in a squeeze bottle. Refrigerate for up to 2 days. (For food safety reasons, do not hold oil any longer than 2 days.) To serve, bring to room temperature; shake well.

Nutrition Facts per serving: 206 cal., 20 g total fat (2 g sat. fat), 0 mg chol., 361 mg sodium, 4 g carbo., 1 g fiber, 4 g pro.

Sage-Brushed Cowboy Steak

A cloudless night, a blanket on the ground, and a thick steak on the grill. What cowboy could ask for more? Pile up skillet-toasted corn and grilled sweet pepper for a simple side dish. To test your steak for doneness, be sure to use a meat thermometer.

Ingredients

1 tablespoon olive oil

3 cups fresh corn kernels or frozen
  whole kernel corn

¼ teaspoon salt

2 beef T-bone or porterhouse steaks,
  cut 1 inch thick

  Salt

  Black pepper

1 small red or yellow sweet pepper,
  halved and seeded

¼ cup snipped fresh sage

2 tablespoons butter or
  margarine, melted

  Large fresh sage sprigs (optional)

⅓ cup queso fresco or
  farmer cheese, crumbled

Prep: 40 minutes **Grill:** 11 minutes **Makes:** 4 main-dish servings

1 In a large skillet heat oil over medium-high heat. Add corn; cook about 10 minutes or until corn is tender and golden brown, stirring often. Stir in the ¼ teaspoon salt. Remove from heat. Cover; keep warm.

2 Arrange medium-hot coals around a drip pan. Test for medium heat over pan. Place steaks on rack over the drip pan. Place sweet pepper halves on the rack directly over coals. Cover and grill steaks and sweet pepper halves until steaks are desired doneness and sweet peppers are tender, turning once. (For steaks, allow 16 to 20 minutes for medium-rare doneness [145°F] or 20 to 24 minutes for medium doneness [160°F]. For sweet peppers, allow 8 to 10 minutes.)(To grill using direct method, allow 11 to 14 minutes for medium-rare [145°F] or 13 to 16 minutes for medium [160°F]. For sweet pepper halves, allow 8 to 10 minutes.)

3 Meanwhile, stir 2 tablespoons of the snipped sage into the melted butter. After turning steaks, brush with melted butter mixture using a pastry brush. Remove steaks and sweet pepper halves from grill.

4 Chop grilled sweet pepper. Stir chopped sweet pepper and remaining 2 tablespoons snipped sage into corn. Just before serving, sprinkle corn with crumbled cheese. Serve corn mixture with steaks. If desired, garnish with additional sage sprigs.

Nutrition Facts per serving: 483 cal., 22 g total fat (9 g sat. fat), 111 mg chol., 317 mg sodium, 29 g carbo., 4 g fiber, 44 g pro.

Menu Options

Grilled Stuffed Green Chiles

These delicious stuffed chiles are served with a fresh tomato salsa. In a pinch, purchased salsa works fine too.

Ingredients

4 large fresh Anaheim chile peppers

  (see note, page 68)

3 ounces soft goat cheese (chèvre)

  or cream cheese, softened

1 cup shredded Colby cheese

  Dash cayenne pepper

  Cooking oil

1 recipe Fresh Tomato Salsa

Prep: 20 minutes **Grill:** 13 minutes **Stand:** 20 minutes
Chill: 1 to 24 hours (salsa) **Makes:** 4 appetizer servings

1 Rinse peppers; pat dry. Cut a lengthwise slit down one side of each pepper. Using a small sharp knife, scrape out seeds and as much membrane as possible without tearing pepper. Leave stems attached.

2 Place peppers on the rack of an uncovered grill directly over hot coals. Grill for 10 to 12 minutes or until skin turns dark and blisters, turning often during grilling. Wrap peppers in foil; let stand 20 minutes. When cool, peel away blackened skin. Be careful not to tear peppers.

3 In a small bowl stir together goat cheese, Colby cheese, and cayenne pepper. Spoon 2 to 3 tablespoons of cheese mixture into each whole pepper. Do not overstuff. Pinch edges together with cheese to seal. Lightly brush peppers with oil. Place peppers, cut sides up, on grill rack directly over medium-hot coals (or place grill basket on rack directly over medium-hot coals). Grill for 3 to 4 minutes or just until cheese melts. Do not turn. Serve warm with Fresh Tomato Salsa.

Fresh Tomato Salsa: In a medium bowl combine 2 cups coarsely chopped tomatoes (2 large); $1/4$ cup finely chopped sweet onion; 1 to 2 small fresh serrano or jalapeño chile peppers (see note, page 68), seeded and finely chopped; 1 teaspoon sugar; and $1/2$ teaspoon salt. Cover and refrigerate for at least 1 hour or up to 24 hours.

Nutrition Facts per serving: 278 cal., 21 g total fat (10 g sat. fat), 36 mg chol., 550 mg sodium, 12 g carbo., 2 g fiber, 13 g pro.

Make-ahead directions: Prepare as above, except do not grilll as in Step 3. Cover and chill for up to 24 hours. Grill as directed.

Shrimp Salsa Verde

To keep shrimp from spinning when turning or from falling into the grill, thread on two skewers as directed.

Ingredients

1 pound fresh or frozen large

   shrimp in shells

16 wooden skewers

2 cups fresh mint leaves

1 cup fresh flat-leaf parsley leaves

1/3 cup olive oil

3 anchovy fillets, drained

2 shallots, peeled and quartered

2 tablespoons water

1/4 teaspoon freshly ground

   black pepper

   Few dashes salt

   Hot cooked rice (optional)

Prep: 20 minutes **Soak:** 30 minutes **Grill:** 6 minutes
Makes: 4 main-dish servings

1 Thaw shrimp, if frozen. Peel and devein shrimp, leaving tails intact. Rinse shrimp; pat dry with paper towels. Meanwhile, soak wooden skewers in enough water to cover for 30 minutes; drain before using.

2 For salsa verde, in a blender container or food processor bowl combine mint, parsley, oil, anchovies, shallots, the water, pepper, and salt until smooth. Set aside.

3 Thread shrimp onto soaked skewers; use 2 skewers for each kabob (1 skewer through head end of shrimp and another skewer parallel to first skewer but through tail end of shrimp) and leave a 1/4-inch space between shrimp. Brush all sides of shrimp with salsa verde.

4 Place shrimp on rack of an uncovered grill directly over medium coals. Grill for 6 to 8 minutes or until shrimp turn opaque and are lightly charred, turning once. If desired, serve shrimp with hot cooked rice.

Nutrition Facts per serving: 245 cal., 15 g total fat (2 g sat. fat), 141 mg chol., 255 mg sodium, 5 g carbo., 3 g fiber, 21 g pro.

Make-ahead tip: The salsa verde can be made up to 24 hours ahead. Cover and refrigerate. Remove from refrigerator 30 minutes before ready to grill the shrimp.

Grilled Brined Pork Chops

Marinating the chops in a brine (salt, sugar, seasonings, and water) for 24 hours—a necessary length of time—yields flavorful and juicy pork. Fennel seeds, ginger, and chile pepper season the brine.

Ingredients

 2 cups hot water

 ¼ cup kosher salt

 ¼ cup sugar

 6 quarter-size slices fresh ginger

 4 cloves garlic, minced

 1 teaspoon fennel seeds

 1 small fresh jalapeño chile pepper,*
      quartered

 2 cups cold water

 4 pork rib chops, cut 1 inch thick

 2 teaspoons olive oil

Prep: 5 minutes **Marinate:** 24 hours **Grill:** 11 minutes
Stand: 5 minutes **Makes:** 4 main-dish servings

1 For brine, in a large bowl combine hot water, salt, sugar, ginger, garlic, fennel seeds, and jalapeño pepper, stirring until salt and sugar dissolve. Add the cold water. Pour brine into a 13×9×2-inch baking dish. Add pork chops. Cover with plastic wrap; marinate in the refrigerator for 24 hours, turning chops occasionally.

2 Drain pork chops in a colander, discarding brine; rinse chops under cold running water. Pat chops dry with paper towels. Brush both sides of each chop with oil.

3 Place chops on the rack of an uncovered grill directly over medium coals. Grill for 11 to 14 minutes or until pork juices run clear (160°F). Transfer to a serving plate; let stand for 5 minutes before serving.

*Note: Because chile peppers contain volatile oils that can burn your skin and eyes, avoid direct contact with them as much as possible. When working with chile peppers, wear plastic or rubber gloves. If your bare hands do touch the peppers, wash your hands and nails well with soap and warm water.

Nutrition Facts per serving: 320 cal., 19 g total fat (6 g sat. fat), 101 mg chol., 440 mg sodium, 1 g carbo., 0 g fiber, 35 g pro.

Comfort Food

Menu

Menu Options

In this menu, you'll find some true comfort foods: the foods we crave after a long, busy day or when life gets difficult. These are the foods that envelop us like a warm blanket; they soothe our souls in their simplicity.

Make these meals as a way of nurturing

yourself and your family. Serve them on a table covered with a small quilt for a homey family meal that is as much a hug as it is sustenance.

ToDo:

Up to 3 Days Ahead

• Prepare Caramel-Orange Sauce for Cranberry Bread Pudding. Cool; cover and refrigerate.

• Prepare aioli for Roasted Asparagus with Tomato Aïoli. Cover and refrigerate.

2 Hours Ahead

• Assemble bread pudding and bake.

• Prepare asparagus through Step 2; set aside.

• Assemble ingredients for Herbed Leek Gratin; prepare through Step 1.

50 Minutes Ahead

• Remove bread pudding from oven; place on wire rack to cool.

• Increase oven temperature to 425°.

• Finish assembling gratin.

45 Minutes Ahead

• Prepare Chicken with Marsala Sauce.

• Bake gratin.

25 Minutes Ahead

• If desired, cook noodles for chicken; snip parsley.

• Let half of the aïoli for asparagus stand at room temperature.

10-15 Minutes Ahead

• Remove gratin from oven; keep warm.

• Increase oven temperature to 450°.

8 Minutes Ahead

• Roast asparagus.

• Toss noodles with butter and snipped parsley.

• If desired, garnish gratin with marjoram.

For Dessert

• Reheat Caramel-Orange Sauce. Serve with bread pudding.

Herbed Leek Gratin

Line up the slender, tender leek halves in an au gratin dish; then add a creamy marjoram sauce and cheesy crumb topping. The combination is delightful.

Ingredients

3 pounds slender leeks

½ cup whipping cream

½ cup chicken broth

½ teaspoon salt

½ teaspoon freshly ground black pepper

3 tablespoons snipped fresh marjoram

1½ cups soft French or Italian bread
     crumbs (about 2 slices)

3 tablespoons grated Parmesan cheese

3 tablespoons butter or margarine,
     melted

     Fresh marjoram sprigs (optional)

Prep: 15 minutes **Bake:** 25 minutes
Oven: 425°F **Makes:** 6 side-dish servings

1 Generously butter a 2-quart au gratin dish or rectangular baking dish. Trim roots off leeks, leaving pieces 4 to 5 inches long with white and pale green parts. Cut the leeks in half lengthwise. Rinse thoroughly under running cold water; pat dry. Arrange leeks, cut sides down, in the prepared baking dish, overlapping as necessary to fit. (Leeks should all be facing the same direction.)

2 In a small bowl combine the whipping cream and chicken broth; pour over the leeks. Sprinkle with salt, pepper, and half of the snipped marjoram. Cover the dish tightly with foil. Bake in a 425° oven for 15 minutes.

3 Meanwhile, in a small bowl combine the remaining snipped marjoram, the bread crumbs, Parmesan cheese, and melted butter. Uncover leeks and sprinkle with bread crumb mixture. Bake, uncovered, for 10 to 15 minutes more or until leeks are tender and crumbs are golden. If desired, garnish with fresh marjoram sprigs.

Nutrition Facts per serving: 237 cal., 15 g total fat (9 g sat. fat), 46 mg chol., 476 mg sodium, 23 g carbo., 2 g fiber, 4 g pro.

Polenta Beef Stew

This stew originated in a region of Switzerland near the border of Italy, where polenta is a commonly used ingredient.

Ingredients

¼ cup all-purpose flour

1 teaspoon garlic powder

1 teaspoon dried thyme, crushed

1 teaspoon dried basil, crushed

¼ teaspoon salt

½ teaspoon black pepper

2 pounds boneless beef chuck steak, cut into 1-inch pieces

2 tablespoons olive oil

¼ cup chopped onion

6 cloves garlic, minced

1 teaspoon snipped fresh rosemary or ¼ teaspoon dried rosemary, crushed

1 14-ounce can beef broth

1½ cups dry red wine

8 ounces boiling onions

5 medium carrots, cut into 1-inch chunks

1 recipe Polenta

½ cup snipped fresh flat-leaf parsley

¼ cup canned tomato paste

Flat-leaf parsley sprigs (optional)

Prep: 25 minutes **Cook:** 2 hours **Makes:** 8 main-dish servings

1 In a medium bowl stir together flour, garlic powder, thyme, basil, salt, and pepper. Coat meat with flour mixture. In a Dutch oven heat oil over medium-high heat. Add half of the meat; cook until browned, stirring often. Transfer meat to medium bowl. Repeat with remaining meat. Return all of the meat to pan. Add chopped onion, garlic, and rosemary. Cook and stir until onion is tender. Add broth and wine. Bring to boiling; reduce heat. Simmer, covered, for 1½ hours.

2 Add boiling onions and carrots. Simmer, covered, about 30 minutes more or until vegetables are tender.

3 Meanwhile, prepare Polenta.

4 To serve, stir snipped parsley and tomato paste into meat mixture. Serve in bowls over Polenta. If desired, garnish with parsley sprigs.

Polenta: In a large saucepan bring 3 cups milk just to a simmer. In a bowl combine 1 cup cornmeal, 1 cup cold water, and 1 teaspoon salt. Stir cornmeal mixture slowly into hot milk. Cook and stir until mixture comes to a boil. Reduce heat to low. Cook for 10 to 15 minutes or until mixture is thick, stirring occasionally. Stir in 2 tablespoons butter or margarine.

Nutrition Facts per serving: 494 cal., 15 g total fat (8 g sat. fat), 105 mg chol., 823 mg sodium, 46 g carbo., 6 g fiber, 36 g pro.

Pork Chops with Roasted Corn Sauce

Extra-sweet varieties of frozen corn will become more brown in roasting than regular sweet corn. The extra sugar in the corn caramelizes to a golden hue, which contributes to the roasted flavor in the sauce.

Ingredients

1 cup frozen extra-sweet whole kernel corn, thawed

1/4 cup chopped red sweet pepper

2 teaspoons cooking oil

3 tablespoons all-purpose flour

1/2 teaspoon cumin seeds, crushed

1/2 teaspoon salt

1/2 teaspoon black pepper

4 pork loin chops, cut 3/4 to 1 inch thick (about 1 3/4 pounds total)

1 tablespoon olive oil

2 tablespoons butter or margarine

1/2 cup chopped onion (1 medium)

2 cloves garlic, minced

2 teaspoons all-purpose flour

1/8 teaspoon white pepper

1 cup half-and-half or light cream

Hot mashed potatoes (optional)

Prep: 35 minutes   **Roast:** 25 minutes   **Oven:** 450°F
Makes: 4 main-dish servings

1 Line an 8×8×2-inch baking pan with foil; set aside. Pat thawed corn and chopped sweet pepper dry with paper towels.

2 Spread corn and sweet pepper in prepared pan. Drizzle with the 2 teaspoons oil. Roast, uncovered, in a 450° oven for 10 minutes; stir. Continue roasting about 15 minutes more or until corn begins to brown, stirring twice. Remove corn and sweet pepper from pan; set aside.

3 Meanwhile, in a shallow dish combine the 3 tablespoons flour, the cumin seeds, 1/4 teaspoon of the salt, and the black pepper. Coat pork chops with flour mixture. In a 12-inch skillet heat the 1 tablespoon oil over medium-high heat. Add chops; cook about 4 minutes or until brown, turning once. Reduce heat to medium; cook, covered, for 8 to 10 minutes more or until juices run clear (160°F). Remove chops from skillet; keep warm.

4 For sauce, in the same skillet melt butter over medium heat. Add onion and garlic; cook for 3 to 4 minutes or until tender. Add roasted corn and sweet pepper. Stir in the 2 teaspoons flour, the remaining 1/4 teaspoon salt, and the white pepper. Add the half-and-half or light cream all at once. Cook and stir until thickened and bubbly. Cook and stir for 1 minute more.

5 To serve, if desired, place chops over mashed potatoes. Spoon sauce over chops.

Nutrition Facts per serving: 457 cal., 28 g total fat (12 g sat. fat), 116 mg chol., 430 mg sodium, 16 g carbo., 2 g fiber, 35 g pro.

Cornmeal Shortcakes with Honey-Roasted Pears

Roasting fruits, like roasting vegetables, enhances their natural sweetness. Use Bosc pears in this out-of-this-world dessert. Bosc pears, available October through April, have a russeted yellow skin and a sweet-tart flavor. They will hold their shape well when baked.

Ingredients

¼ cup honey

¼ cup packed brown sugar

⅓ cup dried tart cherries

3 tablespoons butter or margarine, melted

½ teaspoon ground cardamom or ground cinnamon

4 large Bosc pears, peeled, cored, and sliced ¼ inch thick (about 1¾ pounds total)

1 recipe Cornmeal Shortcakes

Prep: 20 minutes **Bake:** 55 minutes + 8 minutes
Oven: 400°F **Makes:** 4 to 6 servings

1 In a 13×9×2-inch baking pan combine honey, brown sugar, dried cherries, melted butter, and cardamom. Add pears; stir to coat. Bake pears, covered, in a 400° oven about 40 minutes or until tender. Uncover and bake about 15 minutes more or until syrup is thick enough to glaze the pears.

2 Meanwhile, prepare Cornmeal Shortcakes. Remove pears from oven; keep warm. Bake shortcakes.

3 To serve, layer 2 or 3 warm shortcakes and pear slices in 4 or 6 dessert dishes. Drizzle with syrup.

Nutrition Facts per serving: 630 cal., 24 g total fat (14 g sat. fat), 112 mg chol., 357 mg sodium, 102 g carbo., 6 g fiber, 7 g pro.

Cornmeal Shortcakes: In a medium bowl stir together 1 cup all-purpose flour, ¼ cup yellow cornmeal, ¼ cup sugar, and 1¼ teaspoons baking powder. Using a pastry blender, cut in ¼ cup butter until mixture resembles coarse crumbs. In a small bowl combine 1 egg yolk and ¼ cup milk; add to flour mixture, stirring just until moistened. On a lightly floured surface, gently knead dough for 8 to 10 strokes. Divide dough into 12 portions. Pat each dough portion to ¾-inch thickness. Place shortcakes on an ungreased baking sheet. Bake in a 400° oven for 8 to 10 minutes or until golden. Cool shortcakes slightly on a wire rack; serve warm.

Bistro Bound

Menu

Menu Options

Throughout Paris (and, in fact, much of France) it seems nearly every neighborhood has a bistro—a bustling local café or restaurant that serves classic favorites, such as cassoulet and fruit galettes. These are dishes that are never unfashionable, never subject to the culinary whims of the day. The foods of the French bistro are classics that endure because they are so beloved, such as Rack of Lamb with Garlic-Chive Crust and Amaretto Plum Galettes.

Create your own chic bistro: Use a child's chalkboard to write out the menu and set it on a small table and prop it up on a wall if it is large. Surround the board with condiments, tableware, napkins, a small tray, and perhaps flowers in a jar to complete the unstudied, casual look.

ToDo:

Up to 24 Hours Ahead

- Prepare filling for White Chocolate and Berries Napoleons. Cover and refrigerate. Prepare pastry rectangles for napoleons; store in an airtight container.

1¼ Hours Ahead

- Begin soaking mussels for Mussels with Creole Sauce.
- Prepare berries for napoleons. Assemble napoleons; cover and refrigerate.

1 Hour Ahead

- Prepare Rack of Lamb with Garlic-Chive Crust.

35 Minutes Ahead

- Begin preparing Potatoes Anna.

20 Minutes Ahead

- Finish preparing mussels. If desired, serve with lemon wedges.
- Cook potatoes.

15 Minutes Ahead

- Remove lamb from oven. Cover with foil; let stand for 15 minutes.

For Dessert

- If desired, sprinkle napoleons with cocoa powder.

Rack of Lamb with Garlic-Chive Crust

Frenching refers to the way the meat is cut away from the end of the rib so that the bone is exposed. You can ask your butcher to french the lamb for you. But you can easily do it yourself by using a sharp knife to cut away the meat about 1 inch from the tip of the bone. Frenching makes the roasts look impressive.

Ingredients

2 1- to 1½-pound lamb rib roasts

　　(6 to 8 ribs each), with or without

　　backbone, frenched

¼ teaspoon salt

¼ teaspoon black pepper

¾ cup soft bread crumbs (1 slice)

2 tablespoons snipped fresh chives

2 tablespoons snipped fresh parsley

2 tablespoons bottled minced garlic

1 tablespoon butter or margarine,

　　melted

1 tablespoon cooking oil

2 tablespoons stone-ground mustard

1 recipe Potatoes Anna (page 99)

Prep: 20 minutes **Roast:** 25 minutes **Stand:** 15 minutes
Oven: 375°F **Makes:** 4 main-dish servings

1 Trim fat from lamb. Cut the roasts in half (3 or 4 ribs each). Sprinkle with salt and pepper. Wrap the exposed bones with foil. In a small bowl combine bread crumbs, chives, parsley, and garlic; add melted butter and toss until evenly moistened. Set herb mixture aside.

2 In a large skillet heat oil over medium heat. Add half of the lamb; cook about 4 minutes or until brown, turning once. Transfer lamb, meat sides up, to a shallow roasting pan. Repeat with remaining lamb. Spread mustard on meat side of lamb; press herb mixture into mustard. Roast in a 375° oven until desired doneness. (Allow about 25 minutes for medium-rare [140°F] or about 35 minutes for medium [155°F].) Cover with additional foil; let stand for 15 minutes. (The meat's temperature will rise 5°F during standing.) Uncover and remove foil from exposed bones before serving. Serve with Potatoes Anna.

Nutrition Facts per serving: 357 cal., 20 g total fat (7 g sat. fat), 119 mg chol., 411 mg sodium, 8 g carbo., 1 g fiber, 36 g pro.

White Chocolate and Berry Napoleons

These white chocolate cream-filled Napoleons make the wait for the end of the meal interminable. Preparing them is easy with frozen puff pastry. The white chocolate filling can also be made ahead and chilled for up to 24 hours. Easy, yet divine.

Ingredients

½ cup sugar

2 tablespoons cornstarch or ¼ cup
    all-purpose flour

2 cups milk

4 beaten egg yolks

4 ounces white chocolate baking
    squares or white baking
    bars, chopped

2 teaspoons butter or margarine

½ of a 17.3-ounce package (1 sheet)
    frozen puff pastry, thawed

2 cups fresh berries (such as
    raspberries, blueberries, and/or
    blackberries)

    Sifted unsweetened cocoa powder
    (optional)

Prep: 30 minutes **Chill:** 2 to 24 hours **Bake:** 10 minutes
Oven: 425°F **Makes:** 6 servings

1 For filling, in a heavy medium saucepan stir together sugar and cornstarch. Stir in milk. Cook and stir over medium heat until bubbly. Cook and stir for 2 minutes more. Remove from heat. Gradually stir half of the milk mixture into the beaten egg yolks. Add egg yolk mixture to milk mixture in saucepan; bring to a gentle boil. Reduce heat. Cook and stir for 2 minutes more. Remove from heat. Add chopped white chocolate and butter, stirring until melted. Pour into a medium bowl; cover surface of filling with plastic wrap. Chill for at least 2 hours or up to 24 hours. (Do not stir during chilling.)

2 On a lightly floured surface, unfold thawed puff pastry. Using a sharp knife, cut pastry in half crosswise; cut into thirds lengthwise to make 6 rectangles. Transfer rectangles to an ungreased baking sheet. Bake in a 425° oven about 10 minutes or until golden. Remove from baking sheet; cool on a wire rack.

3 To assemble, split pastry rectangles in half horizontally. Place pastry bottoms on dessert plates. Spoon filling and berries over pastry bottoms. Top with pastry tops. If desired, cover and chill for up to 1 hour. To serve, if desired, sprinkle with cocoa powder.

Nutrition Facts per serving: 468 cal., 25 g total fat (7 g sat. fat), 155 mg chol., 233 mg sodium, 52 g carbo., 2 g fiber, 8 g pro.

Make-ahead tip: Cut and bake puff pastry up to 24 hours ahead. Cool on a wire rack. Place in an airtight container. Store at room temperature.

Cheese-Stuffed Pork

Demi-glace (DEHM-ee glahs) is a concentrated brown sauce with a rich, intense flavor. It generally contains beef stock and Madeira or sherry and is often used as a base to make other sauces. You can find demi-glace at specialty food stores.

Ingredients

1   tablespoon butter or margarine

1   cup chopped fresh mushrooms

2   tablespoons finely chopped onion

¼   cup dry white wine

¼   of a 5.2-ounce container
     semisoft cheese with garlic and
     herbs (about ⅓ cup)

1   teaspoon snipped fresh thyme or
     ¼ teaspoon dried thyme, crushed

1¼ cups soft bread crumbs (2 slices)

1   12- to 14-ounce pork tenderloin

    Salt

    Black pepper

1   cup demi-glace

Prep: 20 minutes   **Bake:** 35 minutes   **Oven:** 400°F
Stand: 10 minutes   **Makes:** 4 main-dish servings

1 For stuffing, in a medium saucepan melt butter over medium heat. Add mushrooms and onion; cook and stir for 4 to 5 minutes or until tender. Add wine; boil gently, uncovered, about 2 minutes or until liquid is nearly evaporated. Remove from heat. Add cheese and thyme to onion mixture, stirring until combined; stir in bread crumbs. Set stuffing aside.

2 Trim fat from tenderloin. Using a sharp knife, make a lengthwise cut down the center of the tenderloin, cutting to but not through the other side. Spread tenderloin open. Place tenderloin between 2 sheets of heavy plastic wrap. Working from the center to the edges, pound lightly with the flat side of a meat mallet into a 12×7-inch rectangle. Remove plastic wrap.

3 Spread stuffing evenly over meat, pressing lightly. Starting from a long side, roll up into a spiral, tucking in ends. Tie meat with 100-percent-cotton kitchen string in 3 or 4 places. Place on a rack in a shallow roasting pan. Sprinkle with salt and pepper. Roast, uncovered, in a 400° oven for 35 to 40 minutes or until juices run clear (160°F). Cover; let stand for 10 minutes.

4 Meanwhile, in a small saucepan heat the demi-glace until bubbly. Transfer meat to a cutting board; remove strings. Cut tenderloin crosswise into 8 slices.

5 To serve, divide warm demi-glace among 4 dinner plates; place 2 slices of meat on each plate.

Nutrition Facts per serving: 468 cal., 22 g total fat (8 g sat. fat), 80 mg chol., 1,538 mg sodium, 22 g carbo., 1 g fiber, 39 g pro.

Menu Options

Pork Medaillons with Fennel and Pancetta

A little gourmet, a little down-home, pork medallions and onions experience a bistro-style revival with fresh fennel, Italian bacon, and garlic cream sauce. Round out your meal with steamed green beans or asparagus and winter squash.

Ingredients

1   12-ounce pork tenderloin

¼   cup all-purpose flour

     Dash salt

     Dash black pepper

2   tablespoons olive oil

2   ounces pancetta (Italian bacon) or bacon, finely chopped

2   fennel bulbs, trimmed and cut crosswise into ¼-inch slices

1   small onion, thinly sliced

2   cloves garlic, minced

2   tablespoons lemon juice

½   cup whipping cream

Start to Finish: 30 minutes   **Makes:** 4 main-dish servings

1 Trim fat from pork. Cut pork crosswise into 1-inch slices. Place each slice between 2 pieces of plastic wrap. Pound lightly with flat side of a meat mallet to ¼-inch thickness. Remove plastic wrap.

2 In a shallow dish combine flour, salt, and pepper. Coat meat with flour mixture. In a heavy large skillet cook pork, half at a time, in hot oil over high heat for 2 to 3 minutes or until juices run clear, turning once. (Add more oil, if necessary.) Remove from skillet.

3 For sauce, in the same skillet cook pancetta over medium-high heat until crisp. Add fennel, onion, and garlic; cook for 3 to 5 minutes or until crisp-tender. Add lemon juice; stir in cream. Bring to boiling; return pork to pan. Cook until pork is heated through and sauce is slightly thickened. Transfer pork to a serving platter. Spoon sauce over the pork.

Nutrition Facts per serving: 341 cal., 23 g total fat (10 g sat. fat), 105 mg chol., 175 mg sodium, 12 g carbo., 12 g fiber, 22 g pro.

Menu Options

Amaretto Plum Galettes

Galettes (gah-LEHTS) are another delight we're happy the French invented. What is great about this version is how the pastry dough is simply folded over the fruit filling. You don't have to be a pastry chef and make fancy fluted edges! Be sure to place foil on the baking sheet under the galette before it's baked. It may ooze a little of the juices during baking.

Ingredients

1   cup all-purpose flour

⅛   teaspoon salt

⅓   cup unsalted butter

3 to 4 tablespoons ice water

3   cups thinly sliced pitted plums (about
     6 medium)

⅓   cup granulated sugar

¼   cup slivered almonds

1   tablespoon apple jelly

4   teaspoons amaretto liqueur

2   teaspoons milk

2   teaspoons coarse sugar

     Sifted powdered sugar

Prep: 25 minutes **Chill:** 2 hours **Bake:** 30 minutes
Oven: 400°F **Makes:** 4 servings

1 In a medium bowl combine flour and salt. Using a pastry blender, cut in butter until pieces are pea-size. Sprinkle 1 tablespoon of the ice water over part of the mixture; gently toss with a fork. Push moistened dough to side of bowl. Continue moistening flour mixture, using 1 tablespoon of the water at a time, until all the flour mixture is moistened. Form dough into a ball. Divide dough evenly into 4 portions. Shape each portion into a disk; wrap each disk in plastic wrap. Chill for 2 hours.

2 Line a baking sheet with foil; set aside. On a lightly floured surface, use your hands to slightly flatten 1 portion of the dough. Roll dough from center to edges into an 8-inch circle. Place the dough circle on the prepared baking sheet. Set aside.

3 For filling, in a medium bowl toss together plums and granulated sugar. Mound ¾ cup of the filling to the center of the dough circle, leaving a 2-inch border. Using your fingers, carefully fold the border of dough up and over edge of the filling, pleating the dough as necessary to fit. Sprinkle exposed filling with 1 tablespoon of the slivered almonds. Repeat with remaining dough, filling, and almonds.

4 In a small saucepan heat and stir the apple jelly over medium heat until jelly melts; stir in amaretto. Spoon over exposed filling. Brush pastry with milk; sprinkle with coarse sugar. Bake in a 400° oven about 30 minutes or until crusts are golden. Serve galettes warm or cooled to room temperature. Sprinkle with powdered sugar.

Nutrition Facts per serving: 467 cal., 22 g total fat (11 g sat. fat), 44 mg chol., 79 mg sodium, 64 g carbo., 4 g fiber, 6 g pro.

A Passion for Italian

Menu

Menu Options

Transport yourself to the rolling hills of the Umbrian countryside with this rustic Italian feast. Simple fare becomes an elegant meal when you serve it in your home adorned with special touches unique to Italian cuisine.

Set the stage for everyone's favorite cuisine

with a table adorned in mouthwatering homey Italian style. Purchase colorful cans of Italian goods, such as tomatoes or tomato sauce, and top them with a breadboard. Heap the board high with a selection of Italian breads and small bowls of olives. (Don't forget to place tiny empty bowls on the table for pits!)

ToDo:

Up to 24 Hours Ahead

- Prepare Strawberry Vin Santo Sauce; cover and refrigerate.
- Prepare Dried Yellow Tomato Vinaigrette for Three-Bread Salad; cover and refrigerate.

Up to 6 Hours Ahead

- Prepare génoise for dessert.

1 Hour Ahead

- Pound pork and assemble rolls for Rosemary Pork Rolls with Tuscan Beans. Cover and refrigerate.

35 Minutes Ahead

- Assemble ingredients for Three-Bread Salad; set aside.

25 Minutes Ahead

- Let vinaigrette stand at room temperature.
- Assemble bean mixture for pork; keep warm.

10 Minutes Ahead

- Finish preparing pork rolls. If desired, garnish with fresh rosemary.
- Toss salad with vinaigrette; top with cheese.

For Dessert

- Assemble dessert. If desired, garnish with strawberries.

Menu

Three-Bread Salad

The homemade vinaigrette makes this salad extraordinary. Prepare it ahead of time, then cover and chill it. Splash it over the salad and toss just before serving.

Ingredients

6 cups torn mixed salad greens

2 1-inch slices crusty sourdough
   bread, cut into irregular pieces

1 8-inch whole wheat pita bread
   round, cut into 12 wedges

2 slices pumpernickel bread,
   torn into pieces

1 small red or sweet onion, very thinly
   sliced and separated into rings

1 cup yellow and/or red pear
   tomatoes or cherry tomatoes

1 recipe Dried Yellow Tomato
   Vinaigrette

2 ounces shaved dry Monterey Jack
   cheese or other hard grating cheese

Start to Finish: 25 minutes   **Makes:** 6 appetizer servings

1 In a large salad bowl combine salad greens, sourdough bread pieces, pita wedges, torn pumpernickel, sliced onion, and tomatoes. Drizzle with Dried Yellow Tomato Vinaigrette; toss gently to coat. Top with cheese.

Dried Yellow Tomato Vinaigrette: Place ¼ cup snipped dried yellow or red tomatoes (not oil-packed) in a small bowl. Add 1 cup boiling water; cover and let stand for 10 minutes. Drain tomatoes, reserving ½ cup of the liquid. In a blender container combine tomatoes; reserved tomato liquid; ¼ cup red wine vinegar; 1 tablespoon Dijon-style mustard; 2 teaspoons snipped fresh thyme or ½ teaspoon dried thyme, crushed; ¼ teaspoon salt; and ⅛ teaspoon coarsely ground black pepper. Cover and blend until nearly smooth. With blender running, gradually add ⅓ cup olive oil, blending until combined and slightly thickened.

Nutrition Facts per serving: 269 cal., 16 g total fat (4 g sat. fat), 7 mg chol., 599 mg sodium, 24 g carbo., 3 g fiber, 9 g pro.

Génoise in Strawberry Vin Santo Sauce

Génoise (zhen-WAHZ) is a rich, light-textured cake similar to a sponge cake. It gets its name from its origin of Genoa, Italy. Here the cake is blessed with a luscious sauce that is spiked with Vin Santo, a rich, sweet Italian white wine. Oh, the Italians know how to live!

Ingredients

6 eggs

Granulated sugar

Cake flour or all-purpose flour

¾ cup granulated sugar

⅓ cup extra-light or pure olive oil

(do not use extra-virgin olive oil)

1⅓ cups sifted cake flour or 1¼ cups

sifted all-purpose flour

1 recipe Strawberry Vin Santo Sauce

Sifted powdered sugar

Fresh strawberries (optional)

Stand: 30 minutes **Prep:** 20 minutes **Bake:** 30 minutes
Oven: 350°F **Makes:** 10 to 12 servings

1 Let eggs stand at room temperature for 30 minutes. Grease the bottom and side of a 9-inch springform pan. Line bottom with parchment paper; grease paper. Sprinkle the bottom and side of pan with granulated sugar; dust with flour. Set pan aside.

2 In an extra-large mixing bowl combine eggs and the ¾ cup granulated sugar. Beat with an electric mixer on high speed for 15 minutes. With mixer running, gradually add the oil in a thin, steady stream (this should take about 2 minutes). Turn off mixer immediately after all of the oil has been added. Sift the 1⅓ cups cake flour or 1¼ cups all-purpose flour over egg mixture; fold in until no lumps remain.

3 Pour into prepared pan; place pan on a baking sheet. Bake in a 350° oven for 30 to 35 minutes or until the top springs back when lightly touched. Cool cake thoroughly in pan on a wire rack.

4 To serve, remove cake from pan; remove and discard parchment paper. Cut cake into wedges. Spoon Strawberry Vin Santo Sauce onto dessert plates. Place cake wedges on top of sauce. Dust each serving with powdered sugar. If desired, garnish with strawberries.

Strawberry Vin Santo Sauce: In a blender container or food processor bowl combine 4 cups fresh strawberries, ¼ cup graunlated sugar, and ¼ cup Vin Santo. Cover and blend or process until smooth. Cover sauce and chill up to 24 hours.

Nutrition Facts per serving: 267 cal., 10 g total fat (2 g sat. fat), 128 mg chol., 39 mg sodium, 37 g carbo., 2 g fiber, 5 g pro.

Pasta with Bolognese Sauce

This pasta dish satisfies the craving for a hearty meal and cooks up in 30 minutes.

Start to Finish: 30 minutes **Makes:** 4 main-dish servings

Ingredients

1 28-ounce can crushed tomatoes, undrained

3 8-ounce cans tomato sauce

⅓ cup water

½ teaspoon dried rosemary, crushed

¼ teaspoon crushed red pepper

⅛ teaspoon fennel seeds, crushed

8 ounces shiitake or button mushrooms, coarsely chopped

½ cup chopped onion (1 medium)

1 tablespoon bottled minced garlic

1 tablespoon olive oil

8 ounces ground veal

8 ounces ground pork

½ teaspoon salt

¼ teaspoon freshly ground black pepper

¾ cup dry white wine

1 pound dried castellane or rigatoni pasta

Fresh rosemary sprigs (optional)

Grated Parmesan cheese

1 In a large microwavable bowl combine undrained tomatoes, tomato sauce, the water, dried rosemary, crushed red pepper, and fennel seeds; cover with vented plastic wrap. Microwave on 100% power (high) about 15 minutes or until heated through, stirring every 5 minutes.

2 Meanwhile, in a 12-inch skillet cook mushrooms, onion, and garlic in hot oil for 8 minutes. Add veal and pork; sprinkle with salt and pepper. Cook, breaking up meat with a spoon, until brown. Add wine; gently boil for 2 minutes. Stir in tomato mixture. Bring to boiling. Cover and simmer for 10 minutes.

3 Cook pasta according to package directions.

4 Drain pasta; return to hot pan. Add the sauce; toss to coat. Spoon into a serving bowl. If desired, garnish with rosemary sprigs. Serve with grated cheese.

Nutrition Facts per serving: 815 cal., 22 g total fat (7 g sat. fat), 87 mg chol., 1,726 mg sodium, 115 g carbo., 8 g fiber, 41 g pro.

Mexican Marvels

Menu

Menu Options

Create an impressive Mexican feast full of robust flavors using ingredients found at your grocery store and these great recipes. Choose from beef, pork, shrimp, or chicken dishes to satisfy your craving for foods with a kick.

Add spice to the ficsta with bold, bright colors, such as orange and turquoise. Place small planters filled with succulents and cacti, tomatillos (often referred to as the Mexican tomato), and dried chiles around the table or on a colorful runner.

ToDo:

Up to 24 Hours Ahead

- Prepare Melon Margarita Ice; freeze. Thaw scallops in the refrigerator, if frozen.

Up to 4 Hours Ahead

- Prepare Beef Adobo with Lime Cream through Step 4; refrigerate.
- Prepare Lime Cream; cover and refrigerate.
- Scrape melon ice into glasses; return to freezer.

Up to 2 Hours Ahead

- Prepare Scallop Ceviche through Step 2.

1 Hour Ahead

- If serving, prepare South-of-the-Border Cornmeal Biscuits through Step 3.
- Place biscuits on an ungreased baking sheet. Cover and refrigerate.
- Assemble the ingredients for Spanish Vegetables.

30 Minutes Ahead

- Assemble the remaining ingredients for scallops; stir into scallop mixture.
- If serving, bake biscuits.
- Begin cooking vegetables.

15 Minutes Ahead

- Begin cooking beef.
- If serving, warm tortillas.

For Dessert

- Serve melon ice with cookies.

Menu

Beef Adobo with Lime Cream

Toasting spice seeds, such as the cumin seeds in this recipe, brings out their full flavor. Use this method for other seeds, such as fennel, anise, caraway, coriander, or celery. It's quick and easy to do.

Ingredients

2 dried New Mexico red chile peppers
   or 2 dried ancho chile peppers

1½ cups boiling water

1 teaspoon cumin seeds

1 teaspoon dried oregano, crushed

2 tablespoons sherry vinegar

1 teaspoon honey

¼ teaspoon salt

2 cloves garlic, quartered

4 beef tenderloin steaks, cut 1 inch
   thick (about 1 pound total)

   Nonstick cooking spray

   Salt

1 recipe Lime Cream

1 recipe Spanish Vegetables (see
   recipe, page 126) (optional)

Prep: 25 minutes **Marinate:** 2 to 4 hours **Cook:** 8 minutes
Makes: 4 main-dish servings

1 Remove and discard stems from dried peppers. Cut peppers in half lengthwise; remove and discard seeds. Place the peppers in a small bowl; cover with boiling water. Cover and let stand for 10 minutes.

2 Meanwhile, for marinade, heat a large skillet over medium heat; add cumin seeds. Cook and stir for 30 seconds. Add oregano; cook and stir about 1 minute more or until cumin seeds are toasted.

3 Transfer toasted seed mixture to a blender container or food processor bowl. Drain the peppers, reserving 1 cup of the soaking liquid. Add peppers, reserved soaking liquid, vinegar, honey, the ¼ teaspoon salt, and the garlic to a blender container or food processor bowl. Cover and blend or process until smooth.

4 Place steaks in a plastic bag set in a shallow dish. Pour marinade over steaks; seal bag. Marinate in the refrigerator for at least 2 hours or up to 4 hours, turning bag occasionally.

5 Drain steaks, discarding marinade. Lightly coat an unheated large skillet with nonstick cooking spray. Preheat over medium-high heat. Sprinkle steaks on both sides with additional salt. Reduce heat to medium and add steaks to hot skillet. Cook until desired doneness, turning once. (Allow 8 to 11 minutes for medium-rare [145°F] or 12 to 14 minutes for medium [160°F].) Serve with Lime Cream and, if desired, Spanish Vegetables.

Lime Cream: In a small bowl stir together ¼ cup dairy sour cream, ¼ cup mayonnaise or salad dressing, ⅛ teaspoon finely shredded lime peel, and 1 tablespoon lime juice. Cover and chill until needed (can be made up to 1 day ahead).

Nutrition Facts per serving: 448 cal., 36 g total fat (12 g sat. fat), 88 mg chol., 382 mg sodium, 8 g carbo., 2 g fiber, 22 g pro.

Sensational Greek

Menu

Menu Options

The cuisine of Greece and the Greek Isles is based on a few simple, revered ingredients that are grown and produced with great care in the Mediterranean sunshine. Most important of all may be olive oil, which is part of every meal. Lamb, lemon, garlic, and wine also star in the healthful and lusty foods of Greece.

The ancient olive tree produces the oil that is used not only for cooking, but also for beauty products (soaps and creams) and medicines. Create a stunning centerpiece for your meal by simply placing several types or brands of olive oil in decorative bottles in the middle  of the table. The variations in color—from amber to gold to green—are as beautiful as the flavor differences are fascinating. Complete your edible centerpiece with loaves of crusty bread for tasting the oils and bowls of plump kalamata olives to accompany.

ToDo:

Up to 1 Week Ahead

- Prepare Kourabiedes through Step 2; cool. Store in a freezer container; freeze.

- Prepare Koulourakia Cookies; cool. Store in a freezer container; freeze.

- Prepare Herb-Baked Olives. Cover and refrigerate.

Up to 24 Hours Ahead

- Prepare garlic vinaigrette for Greek Garden Salad. Cover and refrigerate.

- Thaw as many cookies as desired.

50 Minutes Ahead

- Begin preparing Roast Chicken with Olive-Raisin Sauce.

- Assemble the ingredients for Greek Spinach and Rice.

30 Minutes Ahead

- Roast chicken.

- Let vinaigrette for salad stand at room temperature. Prepare salad.

- Cook rice.

- If desired, cook Swiss chard for chicken.

To Serve

- If desired, garnish chicken with olives.

For Dessert

- Sift powdered sugar over Kourabiedes. Serve with Koulourakia Cookies.

Roast Chicken with Olive-Raisin Sauce

When you're in a hurry to present a special entrée, this dish satisfies. Just 25 minutes in the oven and it becomes a fabulous dinner.

Ingredients

2 whole chicken breasts, halved

8 to 12 fresh sage leaves or

    24 sprigs fresh marjoram

¼ teaspoon salt

¼ teaspoon black pepper

2 tablespoons olive oil

½ cup sliced celery

½ cup chopped onion (1 medium)

2 large cloves garlic, minced

½ cup chicken broth

½ cup dry red wine or ⅓ cup broth

    plus 2 tablespoons balsamic vinegar

½ cup pitted and halved mixed olives

    or kalamata olives

½ cup golden raisins

⅛ teaspoon cayenne pepper (optional)

1 tablespoon snipped fresh marjoram

Cooked red Swiss chard (optional)

Whole olives (optional)

Prep: 15 minutes   **Roast:** 25 minutes
Oven: 425°F **Makes:** 4 main-dish servings

1 Loosen chicken skin and place 2 or 3 sage leaves or 6 sprigs of marjoram under the skin of each piece of chicken. Sprinkle chicken with the salt and pepper.

2 Place chicken, skin side up, in a shallow roasting pan. Roast, uncovered, in a 425° oven for 25 to 30 minutes or until chicken is golden brown and juices run clear (170°F).

3 Meanwhile, in a large skillet heat oil over medium heat. Add celery, onion, and garlic; cook until tender. Add the ½ cup broth, the wine, halved olives, raisins, and, if desired, cayenne pepper. Bring to boiling; reduce heat. Simmer, uncovered, about 7 minutes or until slightly thickened. Stir in the snipped marjoram; simmer for 1 minute more.

4 Spoon the sauce over roasted chicken breast halves. If desired, serve with cooked Swiss chard and garnish with whole olives.

Nutrition Facts per serving: 412 cal., 18 g total fat (3 g sat. fat), 95 mg chol., 555 mg sodium, 20 g carbo., 3 g fiber, 35 g pro.

Incredible Indian

While Indian food differs greatly from region to region, all Indian cuisines celebrate the use of spices. Not all Indian food is spicy, however. The use of spices—including fennel, mustard, coriander, cumin, turmeric, and more—predominates throughout India, as does the use of lentils and other legumes.

The many seeds and beans make an appealing tabletop decoration. Pile them directly on an earth-color tablecloth, such as rust, amber, sienna, or mustard yellow, or in vases or votive holders for a conversation starter.

ToDo:

Up to 4 Hours Ahead

• Prepare Creamy Corn Raita through Step 1. Cover and refrigerate.

30 Minutes Ahead

• Remove raita from refrigerator.

• Prepare Indian-Spiced Squash.

20 Minutes Ahead

• Prepare Cumin Rice.

To Serve

• Serve squash over rice. Sprinkle with pumpkin seeds. If desired, serve with chutney and cucumber strips.

• If desired, sprinkle raita with additional sweet pepper. Serve with naan.

Creamy Corn Raita

Raita is a traditional Indian salad that combines yogurt with fresh vegetables. Golden corn and crimson sweet pepper are featured in this version.

Ingredients

2 cups fresh or frozen whole kernel

    corn, cooked, drained, and cooled

½ cup low-fat or fat-free plain yogurt

¼ cup chopped red sweet pepper

2 tablespoons dairy sour cream

¼ teaspoon salt

1½ teaspoons cooking oil

¼ teaspoon cumin seeds

½ teaspoon mustard seeds

1 fresh serrano chile pepper, seeded

    and finely chopped (see note,

    page 68)

    Finely chopped red or green sweet

    pepper (optional)

    Naan (optional)

Start to Finish: 15 minutes   **Makes:** 4 side-dish servings

1 In a medium bowl combine cooled corn, yogurt, the ¼ cup sweet pepper, the sour cream, and salt. In a small saucepan combine oil, cumin seeds, mustard seeds, and chile pepper. Place over low heat and cook about 5 minutes or just until mustard seeds begin to "dance." (Do not overheat or seeds will pop out of the pan.) Stir mustard seed mixture into the corn mixture.

2 Serve immediately. If desired, sprinkle with additional finely chopped red or green sweet pepper. If desired, serve with naan.

Nutrition Facts per serving: 124 cal., 4 g total fat (1 g sat. fat), 4 mg chol., 173 mg sodium, 20 g carbo., 2 g fiber, 4 g pro.

Make-ahead directions: Prepare as above through Step 1. Cover and chill for up to 4 hours. Let stand at room temperature for 30 minutes before serving. If desired, sprinkle with additional sweet pepper and serve with naan.

Curried Vegetable Stew

Serve with hot couscous to soak up all the flavorful juices.

Ingredients

1 tablespoon ground cumin

1 teaspoon ground coriander

1 teaspoon curry powder

¾ teaspoon salt

¼ teaspoon ground allspice

¼ teaspoon ground cinnamon

¼ teaspoon freshly ground black pepper

3 tablespoons olive oil

½ cup chopped onion (1 medium)

1 tablespoon bottled minced garlic

1 tablespoon snipped fresh cilantro

1 small head cauliflower, cut into florets

2 medium zucchini, chopped

1 cup fresh green beans, cut into
    ½-inch diagonal pieces

1 cup canned chickpeas (garbanzo
    beans) (about ½ of a 15-ounce
    can), rinsed and drained

1 cup chopped fresh tomatoes

Hot cooked couscous (optional)

Snipped fresh cilantro (optional)

Start to Finish: 40 minutes **Makes:** 4 main-dish servings

1 In a small bowl stir together cumin, coriander, curry powder, salt, allspice, cinnamon, and pepper; stir in 2 tablespoons water, stirring until smooth. Set aside.

2 In a large skillet heat oil over medium heat. Add onion, garlic, the 1 tablespoon cilantro, and the spice mixture; cook and stir about 1 minute or until onion just begins to soften. Add cauliflower, zucchini, and beans; cook for 2 minutes. Add 1½ cups water. Bring mixture to boiling; reduce heat. Simmer, covered, about 10 minutes or until vegetables are nearly tender. Stir in chickpeas and tomatoes; simmer about 5 minutes more or until vegetables are tender. If desired, serve with couscous and additional snipped cilantro.

Nutrition Facts per serving: 205 cal., 12 g total fat (2 g sat. fat), 0 mg chol., 540 mg sodium, 21 g carbo., 6 g fiber, 7 g pro.

Menu Options

Meatless Days

Menu

Fruit Salad with Star Anise, page 166

Pumpkin Ravioli with
  Vodka-Vanilla Sauce, page 168

Soft breadsticks

Mocha Pots de Crème
  with Ganache, page 170

Menu Options

Caramelized Onion Tartlets, page 172

Vegetarian Skillet Chili,
  page 175

Fresh Vegetable Risotto,
  page 176

Passion Fruit Cheesecake,
  page 177

Meals without meat can be every bit as hearty and satisfying as those with—and many people prefer to consume most of their protein in plant form. The following menu and recipes are especially useful when, as happens more and more, you are cooking for a mixed group of carnivores and vegetarians. No matter what their attitude toward meat, everyone is sure to love the elegant Pumpkin Ravioli with Vodka-Vanilla Sauce or the hearty Fresh Vegetable Risotto.

What better way to celebrate your meatless meal than by decorating your table with nature's glories, such as a green artichoke, bright baby carrots with green stems attached, glorious red tomatoes, and the many other colorful foods available in the produce department. They're every bit as beautiful as flowers, with variations in size, color, shape, and texture that form a compelling arrangement as they pay homage to a luscious meatless meal.

ToDo:

Up to 24 Hours Ahead

- Prepare Mocha Pots de Crème with Ganache. Cover and refrigerate.

Up to 4 Hours Ahead

- Prepare Fruit Salad with Star Anise through Step 2. Cover and refrigerate.

Up to 2 Hours Ahead

- Assemble ravioli for Pumpkin Ravioli with Vodka-Vanilla Sauce. Cover and refrigerate.

30 Minutes Ahead

- Finish preparing ravioli.

5 Minutes Ahead

- Remove star anise from salad. If desired, garnish with mint.

For Dessert

- If desired, top pots de crème with whipped cream and nuts.

Pumpkin Ravioli with Vodka-Vanilla Sauce

Vodka and vanilla in a pasta sauce? Yes! A little bit of vanilla rounds out any sharpness from the vodka. Don't add too much, however, or your dish will take on a dessertlike fragrance.

Ingredients

½ cup canned pumpkin

1 egg yolk

3 tablespoons finely shredded Asiago
    or Parmesan cheese

2 tablespoons fine dry bread crumbs

⅛ teaspoon salt

⅛ teaspoon black pepper
    Dash ground nutmeg or cinnamon

12 wonton wrappers*

1 slightly beaten egg white

1 recipe Vodka-Vanilla Sauce

¼ cup chopped hazelnuts (filberts),
    toasted

Start to Finish: 40 minutes **Makes:** 4 main-dish servings

1 For filling, in a medium bowl stir together pumpkin, egg yolk, cheese, bread crumbs, salt, pepper, and nutmeg.

2 For each ravioli, spoon about 1 tablespoon filling onto center of a wonton wrapper. Brush egg white around edges. Fold diagonally in half to form a triangle; press edges firmly to seal. Cover and set ravioli aside. Prepare Vodka-Vanilla Sauce; keep warm.

3 In a large saucepan bring a large amount of water to boiling. Add ravioli; cook for 3 to 5 minutes or until tender. Using a slotted spoon, lift out ravioli. Drain well.

4 To serve, arrange 3 ravioli on each of 4 dinner plates. Top with sauce; sprinkle with nuts.

Vodka-Vanilla Sauce: In a small saucepan melt 1 tablespoon butter over medium heat. Add 1 shallot, very finely chopped; cook for 3 to 4 minutes or until tender. Stir in 2 teaspoons all-purpose flour. Add ½ cup reduced-sodium chicken broth and 2 tablespoons vodka. Cook and stir until thickened and bubbly. Cook and stir for 1 minute more. Stir in ¼ cup half-and-half or light cream and ¼ teaspoon vanilla bean paste or vanilla; heat through. Stir in ⅛ teaspoon black pepper.

Nutrition Facts per serving: 264 cal., 14 g total fat (5 g sat. fat), 75 mg chol., 430 mg sodium, 23 g carbo., 2 g fiber, 8 g pro.

*Note: Look for wonton wrappers in the supermarket produce section.

Simply Awesome

Menu

Smoked Salmon and
  Avocado Salad, page 180

Sage-Scented Chicken
  with Wine Sauce, page 181

Rice pilaf

Sticky Peaches and Cream, page 182

Menu Options

Cheese 'n' Herb Mini
  Sweet Peppers, page 184

Scallops with Anise-Orange Tapenade,
  page 185

Broiled Portobello Mushrooms,
  page 186

Garlicky Steak and Asparagus,
  page 187

Roast Duck with Raspberry Sauce,
  page 188

Spanish-Style Pork Chops, page 189

Lemon Cream Tartlets, page 190

Lava Baby Cakes, page 191

When you want to serve a spectacular meal—but have no time for preparations—these fast and fabulous dishes are for you. This menu will knock your socks off and allow you a few precious minutes to put your feet up!

In just minutes, you can even decorate your table.
Place leaves or foliage inside a tall or short vase, depending on the leaf. Then add a wide candle to hold the leaves in place. Or tie the leaves to the outside of the vase with string, raffia, or a strip of the foliage. In the autumn, simply pick up the colorful leaves outside your door; wipe them off with a damp paper towel. When foliage season is long gone, you can purchase leaves from your local florist.

ToDo:

Up to 24 Hours Ahead
- Prepare dressing for Smoked Salmon and Avocado Salad. Cover and refrigerate.
- Prepare Cinnamon Cream for Sticky Peaches and Cream up to chilling step. Cover and refrigerate.
- Prepare sauce for Sage-Scented Chicken with Wine Sauce through Step 3.

1 Hour Ahead
- Assemble the remaining ingredients for peaches; set aside.

45 Minutes Ahead
- Bake chicken.

30 Minutes Ahead
- Let dressing for salad stand at room temperature.

20 to 25 Minutes Ahead
- Prepare rice pilaf.
- Reheat and finish wine sauce for chicken (Step 4).
- Assemble salad.

For Dessert
- Finish preparing peaches.

Sticky Peaches and Cream

This sautéed standout is a delicious treat for the family, especially after a stroll on a brisk autumn day. The brown-sugar-glazed peaches are yummy—with or without the cloud of Cinnamon Cream.

Ingredients

2 tablespoons butter

6 medium peaches, peeled, pitted, and sliced, or 6 cups frozen unsweetened peach slices, thawed, drained, and patted dry

2 tablespoons brown sugar

¼ teaspoon ground ginger

6 amaretti cookies or oatmeal cookies

1 recipe Cinnamon Cream

3 tablespoons crumbled amaretti cookies or oatmeal cookies

Start to Finish: 25 minutes   **Chill (cream):** 2 hours   **Makes:** 6 servings

1 In a large skillet melt butter over medium-high heat. Add peaches; cook and stir about 2 minutes or until heated through. Sprinkle with brown sugar and ginger. Cook and stir for 1 to 2 minutes more or until the peaches are coated and caramelized.

2 To serve, spoon about ½ cup of the caramelized peaches into each of 6 bowls. Place a whole cookie next to peaches in each bowl. Spoon about 3 tablespoons of the Cinnamon Cream onto each cookie. Sprinkle peaches with crumbled cookies.

Cinnamon Cream: In a small saucepan combine 3 tablespoons sugar, 2 teaspoons cornstarch, and ¼ teaspoon ground cinnamon. Stir in ½ cup milk. Cook and stir over medium heat until thickened and bubbly. Slowly stir hot mixture into 1 beaten egg yolk. Return mixture to saucepan. Cook and stir about 2 minutes more or until bubbly. Remove from heat. Stir in 2 teaspoons butter or margarine and ½ teaspoon vanilla. Cover surface with plastic wrap. Cool without stirring; chill thoroughly. Just before serving, in a small chilled bowl beat ⅓ cup whipping cream until soft peaks form (tips curl); fold into chilled mixture.

Nutrition Facts per serving: 254 cal., 12 g total fat (7 g sat. fat), 69 mg chol., 72 mg sodium, 36 g carbo., 3 g fiber, 3 g pro.

Dinners for Two

Menu

Menu Options

What could be more romantic than a candlelit dinner for two at home? Simple, unfussy dishes made from fresh ingredients are highly satisfying, yet won't distract you from your time together. Be sure your menu offers a variety of texture, color, and flavor to keep your senses tingling.

Be sure your centerpiece allows room to gaze into each other's eyes—

nothing too high or big that would overwhelm a table for two. Float candles and flowers in a shallow dish of water. As the candles move, they'll cast a glow.

ToDo:

Up to 3 Days Ahead

- Prepare Almond-Praline Chocolate Upside-Down Cakes through Step 3. Cool; wrap in plastic wrap. Cover and refrigerate.

Up to 24 Hours Ahead

- Prepare dressing for Tomato-Feta Salad. Cover and refrigerate.

1 Hour to 1 Hour 10 Minutes Ahead

- Prepare roasted potatoes.

I Hour Ahead

- Assemble salad; refrigerate.
- Prepare asparagus for steaming.

15 Minutes Ahead

- Prepare Beef Tenderloin with Peppercorns.

10 Minutes Ahead

- Steam asparagus.

To Serve

- If desired, garnish beef with pink peppercorns.

For Dessert

- Warm cakes in the microwave oven. If desired, serve with whipped cream or ice cream.

Menu

Beef Tenderloin with Peppercorns

Enjoy the combination of a juicy steak with the piquant taste of ground black pepper. For maximum flavor, fresh-grind the peppercorns in a food processor or coffee grinder. (Be sure to thoroughly clean the grinder after using.)

Ingredients

2 teaspoons cracked whole

   black peppercorns

2 beef tenderloin steaks, cut 1 inch

   thick (about 8 ounces total)

2 tablespoons butter or margarine

2 teaspoons butter or margarine

1 teaspoon all-purpose flour

   Dash salt

   Dash ground black pepper

⅓ cup half-and-half, light cream,

   or milk

1 tablespoon horseradish mustard

   Steamed asparagus (optional)

   Whole pink peppercorns, crushed

   (optional)

Start to Finish: 15 minutes   **Makes:** 2 main-dish servings

1 Sprinkle cracked black pepper evenly over both sides of each steak; press in with your fingers.

2 In a heavy 8-inch skillet melt the 2 tablespoons butter over medium-high heat. Add steaks; cook, uncovered, to desired doneness, turning once. (If steaks brown too quickly, reduce heat to medium.) (Allow 10 to 13 minutes for medium-rare [145°F] to medium [160°F].) Transfer steaks to plates. Cover to keep warm.

3 Meanwhile, for sauce, in a small saucepan melt the 2 teaspoons butter over medium heat. Stir in flour, salt, and the dash black pepper. Add half-and-half all at once. Cook and stir until thickened and bubbly. Cook and stir for 1 minute more. Stir in horseradish mustard. Remove from the heat.

4 If desired, serve steaks on asparagus. Spoon sauce over steaks. If desired, garnish with pink peppercorns.

Nutrition Facts per serving: 360 cal., 28 g total fat (9 g sat. fat), 79 mg chol., 378 mg sodium, 5 g carbo., 1 g fiber, 24 g pro.

Almond-Praline Chocolate Upside-Down Cakes

These tender chocolate cakes, crowned by a praline topping, beg to be served with ice cream or whipped cream. This recipe makes enough for 4 servings. Follow the make-ahead directions to serve the remaining cakes another time.

Ingredients

  2 tablespoons butter

 ⅓ cup packed brown sugar

  2 tablespoons half-and-half or

      light cream

 ¼ cup sliced almonds

 ½ cup all-purpose flour

 ½ cup granulated sugar

  2 tablespoons unsweetened

      cocoa powder

 ½ teaspoon baking powder

 ¼ teaspoon baking soda

 ⅓ cup milk

  2 tablespoons butter, softened

  1 egg

 ¼ teaspoon vanilla

      Whipped cream or vanilla ice cream

Prep: 25 minutes **Bake:** 20 minutes **Oven:** 350°F
Stand: 5 minutes **Makes:** 4 servings

1 Lightly grease four 8-ounce individual soufflé dishes; set aside. For syrup, in a small saucepan melt the 2 tablespoons butter. Stir in the brown sugar and half-and-half. Cook and stir until sugar is dissolved. Divide syrup among prepared custard cups. Sprinkle almonds over the syrup. Set custard cups aside.

2 For batter, in a medium mixing bowl stir together the flour, granulated sugar, cocoa powder, baking powder, and baking soda. Add milk, 2 tablespoons butter, egg, and vanilla. Beat with an electric mixer on low to medium speed about 30 seconds or until combined. Beat on medium to high speed for 1 minute. Gently spoon the batter over the syrup and nuts in the custard cups. Place cups in a shallow baking pan.

3 Bake in a 350° oven for 20 to 25 minutes or until a wooden toothpick inserted near the centers comes out clean. Cool in cups on a wire rack for 5 minutes. Loosen sides and invert the cakes onto dessert plates. Carefully spoon on any almonds that remain in the cups. Serve cakes warm with whipped cream.

Nutrition Facts per serving: 477 cal., 25 g total fat (13 g sat. fat), 111 mg chol., 295 mg sodium, 59 g carbo., 1 g fiber, 7 g pro.

Make-ahead directions: Prepare as above through baking. Cool cakes completely. Wrap cakes individually in plastic wrap. Chill up to 3 days. To reheat, unwrap 2 of the cakes and place on a microwave-safe plate. Cover cakes loosely with waxed paper. Microwave on 100% power (high) for 30 to 45 seconds or until warm. Repeat with remaining 2 cakes.

Winter Green Salad with Herb Vinaigrette

Topped with grapes, walnuts, and a balsamic vinaigrette, this is no ordinary salad.

Prep: 20 minutes **Bake:** 20 minutes **Oven:** 425°F
Makes: 2 appetizer servings

Ingredients

2 roma tomatoes, halved lengthwise and seeded

1½ teaspoons balsamic vinegar

⅛ teaspoon black pepper

Dash salt

3 tablespoons olive oil

1 tablespoon balsamic vinegar

½ teaspoon snipped fresh herb (such as basil, oregano, rosemary, tarragon, or thyme)

⅛ teaspoon salt

Dash black pepper

3 cups mesclun or torn mixed salad greens

½ cup sliced fresh crimini or button mushrooms

¼ cup seedless red and/or green grapes, halved

2 tablespoons coarsely chopped walnuts, toasted

1 Line a small baking sheet with foil; lightly grease the foil. In a plastic bag combine tomatoes, the 1½ teaspoons balsamic vinegar, the ⅛ teaspoon pepper, and the dash salt. Seal bag; shake well to coat tomatoes with vinegar mixture. Arrange tomatoes, cut sides down, on the prepared baking sheet. Bake in a 425° oven for 20 to 25 minutes or until tomato skins are bubbly and dark red but not burned. Set aside.

2 For vinaigrette, in a screw-top jar, combine olive oil, the 1 tablespoon balsamic vinegar, the herb, the ⅛ teaspoon salt, and the dash pepper. Cover; shake well.

3 Arrange the mesclun on 2 chilled salad plates. Top with mushrooms, grapes, and walnuts. Arrange tomatoes to the side of salad. Pour vinaigrette over all. Serve immediately.

Nutrition Facts per serving: 299 cal., 26 g total fat (3 g sat. fat), 0 mg chol., 237 mg sodium, 16 g carbo., 3 g fiber, 4 g pro.

Menu Options

Fiesta Shrimp Appetizers

Spice up cooked shrimp by marinating in lime, cilantro, and Anaheim chile pepper. For even more heat, substitute 2 to 4 tablespoons chopped jalapeño chile pepper for the Anaheim pepper. If you want to shave time off the preparation, use already-cooked, deveined shrimp.

Ingredients

½ pound fresh or frozen large shrimp

in shells

1 clove garlic, minced

¼ teaspoon finely shredded lime peel

2 tablespoons lime juice

2 tablespoons chopped fresh Anaheim

chile pepper (see note, page 68)

1 tablespoon olive oil

1 tablespoon finely chopped green onion

2 to 3 teaspoons snipped fresh

cilantro or parsley

¼ teaspoon sugar

¼ teaspoon salt

⅛ teaspoon black pepper

Lettuce leaves (optional)

Lime wedges (optional)

Prep: 30 minutes **Chill:** 2 to 3 hours **Makes:** 2 servings

1 Thaw shrimp, if frozen. Peel and devein shrimp. Rinse shrimp; pat dry with paper towels. In a medium saucepan bring 2 cups water to boiling. Add shrimp. Simmer, uncovered, for 1 to 3 minutes or until shrimp turn opaque, stirring occasionally. Rinse under cold running water; drain. Set aside.

2 In a plastic bag set in a medium bowl combine garlic, lime peel, lime juice, Anaheim pepper, olive oil, onion, cilantro, sugar, salt, and black pepper. Add cooked shrimp to bag; seal bag. Turn bag to coat shrimp with garlic mixture. Chill for at least 2 hours or up to 3 hours, turning bag occasionally.

3 To serve, drain shrimp; discard the garlic mixture. If desired, serve shrimp on lettuce leaves and serve with lime wedges.

Nutrition Facts per serving: 109 cal., 6 g total fat (1 g sat. fat), 86 mg chol., 279 mg sodium, 3 g carbo., 0 g fiber, 12 g pro.

Lamb Chops with Leek Sauce

Leeks, a member of the onion family, lend a sweet, subtle onion flavor to the sauce. To prepare them, wash well and cut slices from the white base up to about 1 inch into the green stalk.

Ingredients

4   lamb loin chops, cut 1 inch thick

      (about 1 pound total)

      Salt

      Black pepper

1   tablespoon olive oil or cooking oil

2   tablespoons water

2   medium leeks, sliced (⅔ cup), or

      2 green onions, sliced (¼ cup)

1   teaspoon snipped fresh tarragon

      or ¼ teaspoon dried tarragon,

      crushed

⅓   cup whipping cream, half-and-half,

      or light cream

      Hot cooked pasta (optional)

Start to Finish: 25 minutes   **Makes:** 2 servings

1 Trim fat from chops. Sprinkle chops with salt and pepper. In an 8-inch skillet heat oil over medium heat. Add chops; cook for 9 to 11 minutes or until medium-done (160°F), turning once. Transfer chops to 2 dinner plates; cover and keep warm. Drain fat from skillet.

2 For sauce, add the water to the skillet; scrape up crusty bits from the bottom of the skillet. Add leeks and tarragon. Simmer, uncovered, for 1 to 2 minutes or until the leeks are almost tender. Stir in the cream. Bring almost to boiling; reduce heat. Simmer, uncovered, for 1 to 2 minutes or until desired consistency, stirring once. Spoon sauce over chops.

3 To serve, if desired, place chops on top of hot cooked pasta.

Nutrition Facts per serving: 411 cal., 29 g total fat (13 g sat. fat), 166 mg chol., 265 mg sodium, 5 g carbo., 1 g fiber, 37 g pro.

Holiday Happenings

Menu

Menu Options

Host the holidays in glorious style as you ignite your guests with the warm spirit of the day. You'll be greeted with oohs and ahs when you serve a menu that includes such dazzling dishes as Crab Soup, Holiday Beef Tenderloin, or Porcini Rack of Lamb. These are the extraordinary types of dishes that signify to all at your table that this is a special occasion.

Start the meal off with a spectacular

presentation of champagne. Serve the bottle in an ice bowl surrounded with garnet-colored cranberries. To make the ice bowl, fill a plastic bowl with water. Place a smaller bowl inside the large bowl and put a board on top

to keep the bowl in place. Freeze the bowls together, then unmold them. Fill the ice bowl with frozen cranberries, and then place the champagne bottle in the ice bowl. You can even drop a cranberry in each glass to give it color and unforgettable panache.

ToDo:

Up to 24 Hours Ahead

- Prepare Crab Soup; transfer to a bowl. Cover with plastic wrap and refrigerate.
- Prepare Goat Cheese and Chive Potato Cakes through Step 4. Wrap baking pan with plastic wrap. Cover and refrigerate.
- Prepare Almond Cake with Fresh Fruit through Step 3; cover.
- Prepare tomato jam for Holiday Beef Tenderloin. Cover and refrigerate.

1¼ Hours Ahead

- Begin preparing roast beef.
- Cut up fruit for dessert. Cover and refrigerate.

30 Minutes Ahead

- Transfer soup to a saucepan; reheat slowly over low heat, stirring often.

20 to 25 Minutes Ahead

- Remove beef from oven; cover. Let stand.
- Lower oven temperature to 375°; bake potato cakes.
- Reheat tomato jam.
- Cook green beans or Brussels sprouts.

To Serve

- If desired, serve soup with crackers.
- Slice beef and serve with tomato jam. If desired, garnish with rosemary.
- Toss green beans or Brussels sprouts with butter.

For Dessert

- Cut cake into wedges; top with fruit.

Crab Soup

A classic cream soup from South Carolina, this dish was traditionally prepared with fresh crab roe in the spring. The characteristic rosy blush is achieved by substituting paprika for the coral-colored roe.

Ingredients

1 pound fresh or frozen cooked lump crabmeat, flaked and cartilage removed, or one 16-ounce can pasteurized crabmeat

¼ cup butter or margarine

1 cup finely chopped onion (1 large)

½ cup finely chopped celery (1 stalk)

1 shallot, finely chopped

¼ cup all-purpose flour

¾ teaspoon paprika

4 cups milk

2 cups half-and-half or light cream

½ teaspoon salt

1 teaspoon finely shredded lemon peel

1 teaspoon Worcestershire sauce

½ teaspoon black pepper

Few dashes cayenne pepper

¼ cup dry sherry

Prep: 20 minutes **Cook:** 46 minutes **Makes:** 8 side-dish servings

1 Thaw crabmeat, if frozen; set aside. In a Dutch oven melt butter over medium heat. Add onion, celery, and shallot; cook about 5 minutes or until tender.

2 Add flour and paprika; cook for 1 minute. Gradually stir in milk and half-and-half until smooth. Add salt, lemon peel, Worcestershire sauce, black pepper, and cayenne pepper. Bring just to boiling; reduce heat to low. Simmer, covered, for 20 minutes. Stir in crabmeat and sherry. Cover and simmer for 20 minutes more to blend flavors. Do not boil.

Nutrition Facts per serving: 288 cal., 16 g total fat (10 g sat. fat), 105 mg chol., 465 mg sodium, 15 g carbo., 1 g fiber, 18 g pro.

Shrimp and Feta

It's good to have a fairly simple appetizer on hand for the holidays. If you don't have time to make the Garlic Bread Sticks, bagel chips or other purchased crackers will do. If your deli or seafood shop has peeled, cooked shrimp available, it works well here. Purchase 5 or 6 large shrimp per serving.

Ingredients

½ cup bottled olive-oil-and-

    vinegar salad dressing

    or Italian salad dressing

1 teaspoon finely shredded lime peel

3 pounds fresh or frozen large

    shrimp in shells, peeled,

    deveined, and cooked*

¼ cup snipped fresh herbs (such

    as dill, cilantro, and/or parsley)

¼ cup crumbled feta cheese (1 ounce)

    Salt

    Black pepper

    Lime wedges

1 recipe Toasted Bread Sticks

    (optional)

Prep: 30 minutes   **Chill:** 30 minutes to 4 hours
Makes: 18 appetizer servings

1 In a large bowl combine salad dressing and lime peel. Add shrimp. Toss to coat. Cover and chill for at least 30 minutes or up to 4 hours.

2 To serve, combine undrained shrimp, herbs, and feta cheese. Stir gently; season to taste with salt and pepper. Spoon into bowl. Serve with lime wedges and, if desired, Toasted Bread Sticks.

Nutrition Facts per serving: 95 cal., 5 g total fat (1 g sat. fat), 88 mg chol., 195 mg sodium, 1 g carbo., 0 g fiber, 12 g pro.

*Note: To cook shrimp, in a Dutch oven bring lightly salted water to boiling. Add shrimp. Simmer, uncovered, for 1 to 3 minutes or until shrimp turn opaque, stirring occasionally. Rinse under cold running water; drain.

Toasted Bread Sticks: Preheat broiler. Cut one 8- to 12-ounce loaf baguette-style French bread (18 to 24 inches long) in half crosswise with a serrated knife. Carefully cut each piece horizontally into thirds. Arrange bread on a baking sheet. Soften ½ cup butter; spread some of the butter onto 1 cut side of each slice. Broil, buttered side up, about 4 inches from heat for 2 to 4 minutes or until toasted. Turn and broil other side about 1 minute or until lightly toasted. Cool on a wire rack. Break each piece onto thirds. Makes 18 bread sticks.

Nutrition Facts per bread stick: 79 cal., 5 g total fat (2 g sat. fat), 9 mg chol., 119 mg sodium, 7 g carbo., 0 g fiber, 1 g pro.

Baked Ham with Pear Sauce

Baked ham has always been a classic party or holiday food. Today you can buy spiral-cut ham, making serving it a breeze. A luscious pear sauce adorns this succulent ham.

Ingredients

1 cup apple juice or apple cider

1 6-ounce can pineapple juice

¼ cup Calvados or other apple brandy

2 tablespoons brown sugar

10 whole allspice

10 whole black peppercorns

2 bay leaves

1 5- to 7-pound bone-in shank portion spiral-cut ham

1½ pounds Bosc pears, cored and cut into 2-inch pieces

1½ pounds Bartlett pears, cored and cut into 1-inch pieces

3 tablespoons granulated sugar

2 tablespoons cider vinegar

1 1-inch piece fresh ginger

½ of a vanilla bean, split lengthwise

Prep: 30 minutes **Bake:** 1¼ hours **Oven:** 325°F **Broil:** 4 minutes
Stand: 20 minutes + 15 minutes **Makes:** 12 main-dish servings

1 Adjust oven racks to center position and lowest position in oven. In a small bowl combine apple juice, pineapple juice, Calvados, brown sugar, allspice, peppercorns, and bay leaves. Remove rack from a broiler pan; place ham on its side in center of broiler pan. Pour 1 cup of the juice mixture over ham; pour remaining juice mixture into bottom of pan. Bake ham in a 325° oven on center oven rack for 1¼ hours or until an instant-read thermometer inserted in center of ham registers 135°F. Increase oven temperature to broil. Baste ham with pan drippings. Broil ham 4 inches from heat for 4 to 5 minutes or until top is golden brown.

2 Meanwhile, for pear sauce, arrange Bosc pears on a baking sheet. After ham bakes 15 minutes, bake pears on lowest oven rack for 30 minutes. Turn pears and bake about 30 minutes more or until golden brown. In a medium saucepan combine Bartlett pears, granulated sugar, cider vinegar, fresh ginger, and vanilla bean. Bring to boiling; reduce heat. Simmer, uncovered, for 10 to 15 minutes or until Bartlett pears soften but still retain their shape. Remove from heat; cover and let stand for 20 minutes. With a slotted spoon or tongs, remove vanilla bean and ginger; scrape vanilla seeds into pear mixture. (Discard pod and piece of ginger.) Stir baked pears into saucepan.

3 Transfer ham to a cutting board; let stand for 15 minutes. Meanwhile, pour pan juices into a glass measure; remove bay leaves. Let stand for 5 minutes. Skim fat from pan juices. Serve ham with pan juices and pear sauce.

Nutrition Facts per serving: 240 cal., 7 g total fat (2 g sat. fat), 50 mg chol., 644 mg sodium, 27 g carbo., 3 g fiber, 18 g pro.

Porcini Rack of Lamb

A coating of dried porcini (pohr-CHEE-nee) mushrooms lends an intense, woodsy flavor to rack of lamb.

Ingredients

3 large unpeeled shallots

1½ teaspoons olive oil

1¼ cups port wine

3 tablespoons butter

2 teaspoons very thinly sliced garlic

3 tablespoons all-purpose flour

1 14-ounce can reduced-sodium chicken broth

¼ cup prepared demi-glace

1 teaspoon reduced-sodium soy sauce

⅛ teaspoon black pepper

1 ounce dried porcini mushrooms (1 cup)

1 teaspoon salt

1½ teaspoons black pepper

3 1- to 1¼-pound racks of lamb, trimmed

Prep: 30 minutes **Roast:** 45 minutes **Stand:** 10 minutes
Oven: 425°F, 475°F **Makes:** 8 main-dish servings

1 Place shallots in a small baking dish; drizzle with oil. Roast, uncovered, in a 425° oven about 30 minutes or until tender; cool. Peel and cut away root and stem of each shallot.

2 Meanwhile, for sauce, in a small saucepan bring port to boiling; simmer, uncovered, for 8 to 9 minutes or until reduced to ⅔ cup; remove from pan. In same saucepan melt 1 tablespoon of the butter; add garlic and cook for 1 minute. Stir in flour; cook about 1 minute more or until light golden brown. Gradually whisk in reduced port, broth, demi-glace, soy sauce, and the ⅛ teaspoon pepper. Add shallots. Bring to boiling, stirring constantly; reduce heat. Simmer, uncovered, for 2 minutes; strain through a fine sieve. Discard shallots.

3 In a food processor bowl combine porcini, the 1 teaspoon salt, and the 1½ teaspoons pepper. Cover and process to a powder.

4 Arrange oven rack in upper third of oven. Increase oven temperature to 475°. Sprinkle porcini powder onto all meaty sides of lamb. Arrange lamb on the unheated rack of a broiler pan, meaty sides up; roast 15 to 22 minutes or until an instant-read thermometer inserted in center of lamb registers 135°F. Transfer lamb to a cutting board. Cover loosely with foil; let stand 10 minutes. (The temperature of the meat will rise 10°F upon standing.)

5 Meanwhile, in a small saucepan, heat port sauce over medium heat until hot. Cut up remaining 2 tablespoons butter; whisk into hot sauce. To carve racks, cut slices between rib bones. Serve with port sauce.

Nutrition Facts per serving: 450 cal., 34 g total fat (15 g sat. fat), 104 mg chol., 1,073 mg sodium, 12 g carbo., 1 g fiber, 22 g pro.

Make-ahead directions: Prepare through Step 3. Store sauce and porcini powder in covered containers in refrigerator for up to 24 hours.

Menu Options

Santa's Pear Pouches

These pretty little pouches, made from phyllo, are a festive dessert for the Christmas holiday. Cardamom, caramel topping, and pears make up the filling.

Ingredients

3 medium red- or green-skinned pears, cored and thinly sliced (about 3½ cups)

1 tablespoon sugar

1 tablespoon all-purpose flour

¼ teaspoon ground cardamom

⅓ cup butter, melted

8 sheets frozen phyllo dough (9×14-inch rectangles), thawed

¼ cup caramel ice cream topping

Granulated sugar or coarse sugar

Bay leaves (optional)*

Fresh cranberries (optional)

Prep: 30 minutes   **Bake:** 20 minutes   **Oven:** 375°F
Cool: 5 minutes   **Makes:** 4 servings

1 For filling, in a medium bowl combine pears, the 1 tablespoon sugar, the flour, and cardamom. Toss to combine; set aside.

2 Brush four 6-ounce custard cups with some of the melted butter; set aside. Place 1 sheet of the phyllo dough on a cutting board or other flat surface. (Keep remaining phyllo covered with plastic wrap to prevent it from drying out.) Lightly brush the phyllo sheet with some of the melted butter. Place another phyllo sheet on top; brush with butter. Repeat with remaining sheets. Cut stack in half crosswise to form four 9x7½-inch rectangles. Repeat with remaining 2 phyllo sheets to make 4 rectangles total.

3 Gently ease 1 of the rectangles of stacked phyllo into the bottom and up the side of a custard cup (phyllo will hang over edge). Spoon about ¾ cup of the pear filling into center; drizzle 1 tablespoon of caramel topping over pears. Bring phyllo up over filling, pinching together to form a ruffled edge. (If desired, arrange 1 or 2 pear slices so they poke out through top of pouch.) Secure pouch with 100-percent-cotton kitchen string. Brush again with melted butter. Sprinkle with sugar. Repeat with remaining phyllo and filling. Place custard cups in a 15×10×1-inch baking pan.

4 Bake in a 375° oven about 20 minutes or until phyllo is golden brown. Cool 5 minutes in custard cups; remove from cups. If desired, tuck bay leaves under kitchen string and place a few cranberries on serving plate for garnish. Serve warm or cooled.

Nutrition Facts per serving: 364 cal., 18 g total fat (10 g sat. fat), 43 mg chol., 310 mg sodium, 51 g carbo., 4 g fiber, 2 g pro.

*Note: Bay leaves are for decorative purposes only in this recipe. Do not eat them.

Eggnog Pecan Caramel Custard

Fluted aluminum molds give each custard a pretty edge. However, simple custard cups work well too.

Ingredients

⅔ cup sugar

1¾ cups dairy eggnog

3 beaten eggs

⅛ teaspoon pumpkin pie spice

¼ cup chopped pecans, toasted

Prep: 20 minutes **Bake:** 45 minutes **Oven:** 325°F
Chill: 4 to 24 hours **Makes:** 5 servings

1 In a heavy 8-inch skillet cook ⅓ cup of the sugar over medium-high heat until sugar begins to melt, gently shaking skillet occasionally to heat sugar evenly. Do not stir. Reduce heat to low. Cook about 2 minutes or until sugar is melted and golden brown, stirring often with a wooden spoon. Immediately pour caramelized sugar syrup into five 6-ounce custard cups or fluted aluminum molds. Tilt the cups or molds to coat bottoms evenly.

2 In a medium mixing bowl combine remaining ⅓ cup sugar, the eggnog, eggs, and pumpkin pie spice. Using a rotary beater or wire whisk, beat until combined but not foamy.

3 Divide egg mixture among custard cups or molds. Arrange the cups or molds in a 13×9×2-inch baking pan. Carefully transfer baking pan to oven rack. Pour boiling water into the baking pan around the cups or molds to a depth of 1 inch.

4 Bake in a 325° oven for 45 to 55 minutes or until a knife inserted near centers comes out clean. Carefully remove the baked custards from the baking pan. Cool slightly on a wire rack. Cover and chill for at least 4 hours or up to 24 hours.

5 To unmold the custards, loosen edges gently with a knife. Invert a dessert plate over each custard; carefully turn custard cup or mold and plate over together. Lift off custard cups or molds. Sprinkle toasted pecans on top of each custard.

Nutrition Facts per serving: 297 cal., 13 g total fat (1 g sat. fat), 128 mg chol., 94 mg sodium, 39 g carbo., 0 g fiber, 6 g pro.

Caramel Nut Tart

A mixture of nuts with their golden hue creates a stunning dessert for your holiday buffet. A cream cheese pastry makes this tart even more delicious.

Ingredients

1 recipe Cream Cheese Pastry

⅓ cup butter

⅓ cup packed brown sugar

2 tablespoons light-colored corn syrup

1½ cups unsalted mixed nuts

½ teaspoon vanilla

Prep: 25 minutes **Bake:** 38 minutes **Oven:** 450°F, 375°F
Cool: 2 hours **Makes:** 10 servings

1 On a lightly floured surface, use your hands to slightly flatten the Cream Cheese Pastry dough. Roll dough from center to edge into a 16×6-inch rectangle. Wrap pastry around rolling pin. Unroll into an ungreased 13¾×4-inch tart pan with a removable bottom. Ease pastry into tart pan, being careful not to stretch pastry. (Or roll dough from center to edge into a 10-inch circle. Wrap pastry around rolling pin. Unroll into an ungreased 9-inch tart pan with removable bottom.) Press pastry into the fluted sides of tart pan. Trim edges. Line pastry with a double thickness of foil. Bake in a 450° oven for 10 minutes. Remove foil; bake for 8 minutes more. Cool in pan on a wire rack. Reduce oven temperature to 375°.

2 In a heavy small saucepan combine butter, brown sugar, and corn syrup. Bring to boiling over medium heat. Remove from heat. Stir in mixed nuts and vanilla. Pour filling into cooled crust, spreading evenly. Place tart pan on a baking sheet.

3 Bake in the 375° oven for 20 minutes. Cool on a wire rack for 15 minutes; remove sides of pan. Cool completely.

Nutrition Facts per serving: 357 cal., 26 g total fat (11 g sat. fat), 40 mg chol., 180 mg sodium, 27 g carbo., 3 g fiber, 6 g pro.

Cream Cheese Pastry: In a bowl stir together 1¼ cups all-purpose flour and ⅛ teaspoon salt. Cut in one 3-ounce package cold cream cheese and ¼ cup cold butter until pieces are pea-size. Using a fork, stir in 2 to 3 tablespoons ice water and 1 teaspoon cider vinegar until all dough is moistened. Using your fingers, gently knead the dough just until a ball forms. Flatten dough into a disk.

Weeknight Wonders

Even on those days when you can't seem to stop long enough to think, you can get a good home-cooked meal on the table—all it takes is a little weeknight wizardry! Turn to the magic of good, quick recipes like the ones for the Easy Beef Stroganoff and Salmon with Pesto Mayonnaise on the following pages. When you've made any of these recipes once, you'll see they're so simple and tasty, they'll become part of your regular weeknight repertoire.

Don't think that just because you're feeling

harried you don't have time to create a lovely table setting. Treasure a keepsake weeknight tablecloth made by your children for years to come. Give them crayons or permanent markers and an inexpensive white cloth and let them express themselves!

ToDo:

Up to 2 Weeks Ahead

- Prepare Peanut Butter Chocolate Chip Bars; cool. Place in freezer container; freeze.

1 Hour Ahead

- Thaw as many bars as desired for dessert.
- Assemble Orange Dream Fruit Salad. Cover and refrigerate.
- Assemble Cheese Garlic Biscuits. Drop onto baking sheet. Cover and refrigerate.

30 Minutes Ahead

- Prepare Easy Beef Stroganoff.

20 Minutes Ahead

- Preheat oven for biscuits.

10 Minutes Ahead

- Bake biscuits.

227

Weeknight Steak with Vegetables

Roasting the vegetables gives them a robust flavor and keeps most of the work for this dish in one pan. Your favorite mashed potatoes make a tempting and delicious plate mate.

Ingredients

2 tablespoons olive oil

2 medium zucchini and/or yellow
   summer squash, cut into
   1-inch chunks

1 large onion, cut into thick wedges

2 stalks celery, cut into 1-inch slices

3 cloves garlic, peeled

1 teaspoon dried rosemary, crushed

1 pound boneless beef sirloin steak,
   cut ¾ inch thick

Salt

Black pepper

½ cup Zinfandel or other fruity
   dry red wine

1 14½-ounce can diced tomatoes
   with basil, oregano, and
   garlic, undrained

Start to Finish: 30 minutes **Makes:** 4 main-dish servings

1 In a large skillet heat 1 tablespoon of the oil over medium heat. Add the zucchini, onion, celery, garlic, and rosemary; cook for 6 to 7 minutes or just until vegetables are crisp-tender, stirring occasionally. Remove from skillet.

2 Cut steak into 4 serving-size pieces. Add remaining 1 tablespoon oil to skillet. Add steak to hot skillet. Season with salt and pepper. Cook over medium-high heat for 4 to 6 minutes or until medium-rare (145°F), turning once. (Meat doneness will increase slightly during standing time.) Remove meat from skillet; cover and keep warm.

3 Add wine to the skillet, stirring to scrape up brown bits. Add the undrained tomatoes. Bring to boiling. Boil gently, uncovered, about 5 minutes or until slightly thickened. Return vegetables to skillet. Cook and stir just until mixture is heated through. Spoon vegetable mixture over steak.

Nutrition Facts per serving: 388 cal., 23 g total fat (7 g sat. fat), 74 mg chol., 362 mg sodium, 16 g carbo., 3 g fiber, 24 g pro.

Ham with Fruit Salsa

Mango-apple salsa is a refreshing fruit topper used to sweeten up the salty taste of ham.

Ingredients

1   mango, peeled and diced

½   Granny Smith apple, cored and diced

1   tablespoon snipped fresh cilantro

2   teaspoons lime juice

1½ teaspoons sugar

Few dashes salt

1   teaspoon olive oil

½   teaspoon ground cumin

¼   teaspoon freshly ground

black pepper

1   1¾- to 2-pound bone-in,

thick-cut cooked ham steak

(about ¾ inch thick)

Hot cooked rice (optional)

Snipped fresh cilantro (optional)

Start to Finish: 15 minutes   **Makes:** 4 to 6 main-dish servings

1 For salsa, in a medium bowl combine mango, apple, the 1 tablespoon cilantro, the lime juice, 1 teaspoon of the sugar, and the salt. Set aside.

2 In a small bowl combine oil, cumin, the remaining ½ teaspoon sugar, and pepper. Brush oil mixture on both sides of ham. Preheat stove top grill pan or large nonstick skillet over medium-high heat. Add ham; cook for 8 to 10 minutes or until heated through, turning once.

3 To serve, top ham with salsa. If desired, serve with hot cooked rice and garnish with additional cilantro.

Nutrition Facts per serving: 280 cal., 12 g total fat (4 g sat. fat), 74 mg chol., 1,909 mg sodium, 13 g carbo., 1 g fiber, 29 g pro.

Make-ahead directions: Prepare as above through Step 1. Cover and chill up to 24 hours. To serve, continue as above in Steps 2 and 3.

Health Wise

Menu

Menu Options

Nurture friends and family in the most caring way of all when you prepare a meal that is as healthful as it is delicious. Don't feel compelled to tell them they're eating healthfully—they'll love dishes such as Chicken with Braised Spinach and Leek, Pork Medaillons with Pear-Maple Sauce, Nectarine Tart, and Berry Clafouti.

Bottled waters and teas are the drinks of choice for the health-minded set. Buy lots of flavorful drinks and serve them in an ice-filled container. With all the new flavors, you'll want to try several! Look for the most variety at health food stores. Or brew fruit and flower teas, such as hibiscus, flavor them with fresh mint and honey, and serve the drink in pitchers filled with lots of ice. Float sliced fruit (sangria style) in the pitchers for added appeal—and nutrients.

ToDo:

Up to 24 Hours Ahead

- Prepare White Bean and Tomato Bruschetta through Step 3. Cover and refrigerate tomato and bean mixtures. Place toasted baguette slices in an airtight container; store at room temperature.

1 Hour 10 Minutes Ahead

- Prepare Berry Clafouti; preheat oven.

55 Minutes Ahead

- Bake clafouti.

45 Minutes Ahead

- Assemble bruschetta; set aside.

40 Minutes Ahead

- Begin preparing Chicken with Braised Spinach and Leek.

30 to 35 Minutes Ahead

- Remove clafouti from oven to wire rack.
- Preheat broiler.

20 Minutes Ahead

- Broil chicken and prepare spinach and leek mixture. Cover and keep vegetable mixture warm.

5 Minutes Ahead

- Remove chicken from broiler. Cover; keep warm.
- Broil bruschetta. If desired, garnish with watercress.

For Dessert

- Sprinkle clafouti with powdered sugar.

White Bean and Tomato Bruschetta

Almost everything for this appetizer can be made ahead. Assemble and heat the bruschetta just before serving. Then relax.

Ingredients

2 tablespoons oil-packed

    dried tomatoes

½ cup snipped fresh watercress

    or flat-leaf parsley

2 tablespoons pine nuts, toasted

1 cup canned white kidney (cannellini)

    beans, rinsed and drained

1 tablespoon milk

2 to 3 teaspoons lemon juice

1 teaspoon snipped fresh thyme or

    ¼ teaspoon dried thyme, crushed

¼ teaspoon salt

¼ teaspoon freshly ground

    black pepper

2 cloves garlic, cut up

12 ½-inch slices baguette-style

    French bread

    Watercress sprigs (optional)

Start to Finish: 30 minutes **Makes:** 4 to 6 servings

1 Preheat broiler. Drain tomatoes, reserving oil; finely snip tomatoes. In a small bowl combine snipped tomatoes, 1 teaspoon of the reserved oil, the ½ cup watercress, and the pine nuts; set tomato mixture aside.

2 In a food processor bowl or blender container combine another 1 teaspoon of the reserved oil, the beans, milk, lemon juice, thyme, salt, pepper, and garlic. Cover and process or blend until smooth. Set bean mixture aside.

3 Place bread slices on a baking sheet. Broil 4 inches from the heat for 45 to 60 seconds on each side or until lightly toasted. Remove from oven; cool slightly.

4 Place about 1 tablespoon of the bean mixture on each of the toasted bread slices, spreading evenly to edges. Broil 4 inches from heat about 1 minute or until bean mixture is warm. Remove from oven. Top each with some of the tomato mixture. If desired, garnish with watercress sprigs. Serve immediately.

Nutrition Facts per serving: 147 cal., 6 g total fat (1 g sat. fat), 0 mg chol., 377 mg sodium, 21 g carbo., 4 g fiber, 7 g pro.

Make-ahead directions: Prepare as above through Step 3. Cover and chill tomato and bean mixtures up to 24 hours. Place toasted baguette slices in an airtight container and store at room temperature for up to 24 hours. Assemble and serve as above in Step 4.

Berry Clafouti

Once again, the French are responsible for a masterpiece dessert. Clafouti (kla-foo-TEE) is fruit that is topped with a batter and baked. Cherries are the classic fruit of choice but are by no means the only fruit to use. Try chopped peaches, plums, or pears, if you like.

Ingredients

2 slightly beaten egg whites

1 slightly beaten egg

3 tablespoons granulated sugar

1 tablespoon honey

1 tablespoon fruit-flavored liqueur (such

as orange or raspberry liqueur)

or ½ teaspoon rum extract plus

2 tablespoons orange juice

½ teaspoon vanilla

Dash salt

¾ cup plain fat-free yogurt

½ cup all-purpose flour

3 cups fresh raspberries, blueberries,

and/or sliced strawberries

2 teaspoons sifted powdered

sugar (optional)

Prep: 15 minutes **Bake:** 20 minutes **Oven:** 375°F
Cool: 30 minutes **Makes:** 6 servings

1 In a large mixing bowl combine egg whites, whole egg, granulated sugar, honey, liqueur, vanilla, and salt; beat with a wire whisk or an electric mixer on low speed until light and frothy. Stir in the yogurt until mixture is smooth. Add flour; beat until mixture is smooth.

2 Grease six 6-ounce individual quiche dishes. Arrange berries in bottom of dishes. Spoon batter over berries. (Batter will not cover berries completely.) Bake in a 375° oven for 20 to 25 minutes or until centers appear set when shaken. Cool on a wire rack for 30 minutes.

3 Just before serving, if desired, sprinkle with powdered sugar.

Nutrition Facts per serving: 141 cal., 1 g total fat (0 g sat. fat), 36 mg chol., 76 mg sodium, 27 g carbo., 3 g fiber, 6 g pro.

Pork Medaillons with Pear-Maple Sauce

Juicy pears, tart cherries, and maple syrup scented with rosemary and thyme give this appealing entrée a distinctive flavor.

Ingredients

1 12- to 16-ounce pork tenderloin

2 teaspoons snipped fresh rosemary
     or ½ teaspoon dried rosemary,
     crushed

1 teaspoon snipped fresh thyme or
     ¼ teaspoon dried thyme, crushed

¼ teaspoon salt

¼ teaspoon black pepper

1 tablespoon olive oil or cooking oil

2 medium pears, thinly sliced

¼ cup pure maple syrup or maple-
     flavored syrup

2 tablespoons dried tart cherries,
     halved

2 tablespoons dry white wine
     or apple juice

Start to Finish: 25 minutes **Makes:** 4 main-dish servings

1 Trim fat from pork. Cut pork into ¼-inch slices. In a medium bowl combine rosemary, thyme, salt, and pepper. Add pork slices; toss to coat. In a large skillet cook pork, half at a time, in hot oil for 2 to 3 minutes or until pork is done and juices run clear, turning once. Remove pork from skillet; set aside.

2 In the same skillet combine the pears, maple syrup, dried cherries, and wine. Bring mixture to boiling; reduce heat. Boil gently, uncovered, about 3 minutes or just until the pears are tender. Return pork to skillet; heat through.

3 To serve, use a slotted spoon to transfer pork to a warm serving platter. Spoon the pear mixture over pork.

Nutrition Facts per serving: 255 cal., 7 g total fat (2 g sat. fat), 60 mg chol., 179 mg sodium, 29 g carbo., 3 g fiber, 19 g pro.

Salmon with Apricot Sauce

A fruity hot-pepper sauce gives the salmon a happy zap of flavor.

Ingredients

4 fresh or frozen salmon or halibut
   steaks, cut ¾ inch thick (about
   1¼ pounds total)

4 fresh apricots, halved and pitted,*
   or 8 dried apricot halves

½ cup apricot nectar

⅓ cup apricot preserves

3 tablespoons sliced green onions

1½ teaspoons snipped fresh oregano
   or ½ teaspoon dried
   oregano, crushed

⅛ teaspoon salt

   Few dashes bottled hot
   pepper sauce

1 tablespoon olive oil

1 to 2 teaspoons bottled hot
   pepper sauce

   Salt

   Black pepper

   Nonstick cooking spray

   Fresh oregano sprigs (optional)

Prep: 25 minutes **Grill:** 6 minutes **Makes:** 4 main-dish servings

1 Thaw salmon, if frozen. Rinse salmon; pat dry with paper towels. Set aside. Cut up fresh apricots; set aside. (Or if using dried apricots, place in a small bowl and cover with boiling water. Let stand until needed.)

2 For sauce, in a small saucepan combine apricot nectar, preserves, green onions, oregano, and the ⅛ teaspoon salt. Bring just to boiling, stirring frequently; reduce heat. Boil gently, uncovered, about 8 minutes or until sauce thickens slightly. Remove from heat; reserve ¼ cup of the sauce to brush on fish. In a small bowl combine remaining sauce, apricots, and the few dashes hot pepper sauce. (If using dried apricots, drain well before adding to sauce mixture.) Cover sauce and keep warm.

3 In a small bowl stir together the olive oil and the 1 to 2 teaspoons hot pepper sauce. Brush both sides of fish with the oil mixture. Sprinkle fish lightly with additional salt and black pepper.

4 Coat an unheated grill rack of an uncovered grill with nonstick cooking spray. Place salmon on the prepared rack directly over medium coals. Grill for 6 to 9 minutes or just until fish flakes easily when tested with a fork, turning once halfway through grilling. Brush salmon with the reserved ¼ cup sauce during the last 2 to 3 minutes of grilling time. Discard any remaining sauce.

5 Transfer salmon to serving platter. Spoon chunky apricot sauce over salmon. If desired, garnish with oregano sprigs.

Nutrition Facts per serving: 304 cal., 8 g total fat (1 g sat. fat), 73 mg chol., 260 mg sodium, 27 g carbo., 2 g fiber, 29 g pro.

*Note: If desired, grill the fresh apricot halves, cut sides down, over medium coals a few minutes or just until they begin to brown. Cut up the apricots and add to the sauce in Step 2.

Stuffed Chicken Breasts with Apple-Thyme Sauce

This recipe gives you a couple of make-ahead options. Make the chicken rolls and sauce ahead. At the last minute, heat the sauce and continue as directed. The chicken may need just an extra minute or two in the oven.

Ingredients

8 skinless, boneless chicken breast
   halves (about 2 pounds total)

   Salt

   Black pepper

2 tablespoons olive oil

4 cloves garlic, minced

1 10-ounce package frozen chopped
   spinach, thawed and well drained

2/3 cup dried currants or raisins

1/3 cup pine nuts, toasted

1 1/3 cups reduced-sodium chicken broth

1/2 cup apple juice or apple cider

4 teaspoons cornstarch

1 tablespoon snipped fresh thyme or
   3/4 teaspoon dried thyme, crushed

1 tablespoon butter or margarine

Prep: 30 minutes   **Bake:** 25 minutes   **Oven:** 375°F
Makes: 8 main-dish servings

1 Place each breast half between 2 pieces of plastic wrap. Pound lightly with the flat side of a meat mallet to 1/4-inch thickness. Remove plastic wrap. Sprinkle lightly with salt and pepper; set aside.

2 In a medium skillet heat 2 teaspoons of the olive oil over medium heat; add garlic. Cook and stir about 30 seconds or until golden brown. Remove from heat. Stir in well-drained spinach, 1/3 cup of the currants, and half of the pine nuts. Season lightly with salt and pepper.

3 Divide spinach mixture among chicken breasts. Starting from a long side, roll up each chicken breast into a spiral, folding in ends.

4 Lightly grease a 3-quart rectangular baking dish. Place chicken roll-ups, seam sides down, in prepared baking dish. Brush with remaining olive oil. Sprinkle with additional pepper. (Cover and refrigerate for up to 4 hours.) Bake, uncovered, in a 375° oven about 25 minutes or until chicken is no longer pink and juices run clear.

5 Meanwhile, for sauce, in a small saucepan gradually stir chicken broth and apple juice into cornstarch. Add remaining 1/3 cup currants and the dried thyme, if using. Cook and stir until thickened and bubbly. Cook and stir for 2 minutes more. Remove from heat. (Cover and refrigerate for up to 4 hours. Reheat before serving.) Stir in remaining pine nuts, the butter, and the fresh thyme, if using.

6 To serve, diagonally slice each chicken breast into 1/2-inch slices. Arrange chicken slices on dinner plates; drizzle with a little sauce. Pass remaining sauce.

Nutrition Facts per serving: 272 cal., 10 g total fat (2 g sat. fat), 70 mg chol., 358 mg sodium, 17 g carbo., 2 g fiber, 30 g pro.

Menu Options

Basmati Rice Pilaf with Toasted Pecans

Basmati rice is famous for its nutty aroma, which some say is reminiscent of popcorn. Serve alongside the entrées featured in this chapter.

Ingredients

2 cloves garlic, minced

2 teaspoons olive oil

2½ cups reduced-sodium chicken broth

1 cup basmati rice

4 ounces crimini or button

    mushrooms, sliced (1½ cups)

½ cup thinly sliced green onions (4)

¼ cup chopped red sweet pepper

2 teaspoons finely shredded

    lemon peel

¼ teaspoon salt

⅛ teaspoon freshly ground black

    pepper

2 tablespoons chopped pecans,

    toasted

    Lemon slices (optional)

Prep: 20 minutes   **Cook:** 20 minutes   **Makes:** 6 side-dish servings

1 In a medium saucepan cook garlic in hot oil for 30 seconds. Add the chicken broth and uncooked rice. Bring to boiling; reduce heat. Simmer, covered, for 10 minutes.

2 Stir in mushrooms, green onions, sweet pepper, lemon peel, salt, and black pepper. Cover; cook for 10 to 15 minutes more or until liquid is absorbed and rice is tender. Stir in pecans. If desired, garnish with lemon slices.

Nutrition Facts per serving: 147 cal., 4 g total fat (0 g sat. fat), 0 mg chol., 258 mg sodium, 25 g carbo., 2 g fiber, 4 g pro.

Nectarine Tart

The filling in this low-fat dessert tastes deceivingly rich. Fat-free cream cheese is the secret. For a pretty finish, arrange the nectarine slices and blueberries in a pinwheel design before glazing with the apricot spread.

Ingredients

1 cup all-purpose flour

¼ teaspoon salt

¼ cup butter

4 to 5 tablespoons cold water

1 8-ounce package fat-free cream cheese (block style), softened

¼ cup sugar

1 teaspoon vanilla

4 or 5 nectarines or peeled peaches, sliced, or one 16-ounce package frozen unsweetened peach slices, thawed and drained

½ cup blueberries

½ cup low-calorie apricot spread

Prep: 40 minutes **Bake:** 12 minutes **Oven:** 450°F
Chill: 2 to 3 hours **Makes:** 12 servings

1 In a medium bowl combine flour and salt. Using a pastry blender, cut in butter until pieces are pea-size. Sprinkle 1 tablespoon of the water over part of the mixture; gently toss with a fork. Push moistened dough to side of bowl. Repeat moistening dough, using 1 tablespoon of the water at a time, until all of the dough is moistened. Form into a ball.

2 On a lightly floured surface, flatten dough. Roll from center to edge into a 12-inch circle. Roll dough around a rolling pin and place into a 10-inch tart pan with a removable bottom. Ease into pan, being careful not to stretch pastry. Press pastry about ½ inch up the side of the pan. Prick the bottom well with a fork. Bake in a 450° oven for 12 to 15 minutes or until golden brown. Cool in pan on a wire rack. Remove side of tart pan.

3 Meanwhile, in a medium mixing bowl combine the cream cheese, sugar, and vanilla. Beat with an electric mixer on medium speed until smooth. Spread over the cooled pastry. Arrange the nectarines or peaches over cream cheese layer. Sprinkle with the blueberries.

4 In a small saucepan heat the apricot spread until melted; cut up any large pieces. Spoon the melted spread over fruit. Chill for at least 2 hours or up to 3 hours.

Nutrition Facts per serving: 156 cal., 4 g total fat (3 g sat. fat), 13 mg chol., 90 mg sodium, 27 g carbo., 1 g fiber, 4 g pro.

Citrus Compote with Pomegranate

One of the keys to this dessert is to remove all the membranes and bitter-tasting pith. See note, below right, on how to do it.

Ingredients

¾ cup dry white wine

2 tablespoons brown sugar

2 tablespoons honey

1 tablespoon dry sherry (optional)

6 pink grapefruit, peeled and

    sectioned*

2 navel oranges, peeled and

    sectioned*

    Seeds and juice from

        1 pomegranate or ⅓ cup dried

        cherries or cranberries

Prep: 30 minutes **Chill:** 1 to 2 hours + 20 minutes **Makes:** 6 servings

1 For sauce, in a small saucepan combine wine, brown sugar, honey, and, if desired, sherry. Cook over medium-high heat just until boiling, stirring until brown sugar is dissolved. Remove from heat. Cover and chill for at least 1 hour or up to 2 hours.

2 Divide grapefruit and orange sections among 6 parfait glasses or dessert bowls. Sprinkle pomegranate seeds and juice over fruit. Spoon sauce over all. Cover and chill for 20 minutes before serving.

Nutrition Facts per serving: 161 cal., 0 g total fat (0 g sat. fat), 0 mg chol., 4 mg sodium, 36 g carbo., 3 g fiber, 2 g pro.

*Note: To section the fruit, cut peels from grapefruit and oranges by slicing ½ inch off top and bottom of each. Remove remaining peel by standing fruit on cut bottoms and slicing peel from top to bottom, moving the knife with the shape of the fruit. This should remove most of the white membrane. Next, hold each piece of fruit in one hand and carefully cut with a thin-bladed knife to free segments from their membranes. Do this by cutting as close to each segment-dividing membrane as possible.

Party of 12

Menu

Menu Options

The trick to feeding a large group is picking your recipes wisely. Don't choose dishes that require a lot of last-minute, time-consuming attention. The following menu gives you great party food you can make in quantity, and get a lot done in advance, so you can relax and enjoy your own party.

Buffets are always kindest to the party host.

Be sure to dress your buffet table with your imagination. Adorn it with cloches or cake covers and fresh fruit—anything that adds height and color and makes your table look laden with more than everything a hungry guest could ever want.

ToDo:

Up to 24 Hours Ahead

- Prepare White Chocolate Berry Cheesecake and raspberry sauce. Cover and refrigerate.

- Thaw shrimp in the refrigerator, if frozen.

3½ Hours Ahead

- Peel and devein shrimp for Old City BBQ Shrimp; place in baking pan. Cover and refrigerate.

2½ to 3¾ Hours Ahead

- Begin preparing Basil-Stuffed Beef.

2 to 2¾ Hours Ahead

- Begin roasting beef.

25 Minutes Ahead

- Finish assembling shrimp; set aside.

- Cook carrots.

15 Minutes Ahead

- Remove beef from oven. Cover and let stand.

- Increase oven temperature to 350°; bake shrimp.

To Serve

- Toss carrots with butter.

For Dessert

- Serve cheesecake with raspberry sauce. If desired, serve with fresh raspberries and garnish with mint.

White Chocolate Berry Cheesecake

Swirl some of the ruby-red sauce, made with frozen raspberries, through the cheesecake and serve the rest of the sauce drizzled on the plate under each serving. Delicious.

Ingredients

1   12-ounce package frozen slightly

     sweetened raspberries

⅓ cup sugar

1   teaspoon cornstarch

1½ cups crushed chocolate wafers

     (about 25)

3   tablespoons butter, melted

1   6-ounce package white chocolate

     baking squares or white baking

     bars, chopped

3   8-ounce packages cream cheese,

     softened

½ cup sugar

3   eggs

Prep: 40 minutes **Bake:** 40 minutes **Oven:** 350°F **Cool:** 45 minutes
Chill: 4 to 24 hours **Makes:** 12 to 16 servings

1 For raspberry sauce, thaw berries; do not drain. Place half of the berries in a blender container or food processor bowl. Cover and blend or process until berries are smooth. Press berries through a fine-mesh sieve; discard seeds. Repeat with remaining berries. (You should have 1 to 1¼ cups sieved puree.) In a small saucepan stir together the ⅓ cup sugar and the cornstarch. Add sieved berries. Cook and stir over medium heat until thickened and bubbly. Cook and stir for 2 minutes more. Remove from heat. Set aside 2 tablespoons of the sauce. Cover and chill the remaining sauce until serving time.

2 For crumb crust, in a medium bowl combine crushed chocolate wafers and melted butter. Press into the bottom of a 9-inch springform pan. Set aside. In a small saucepan melt white chocolate over very low heat, stirring constantly. Set aside to cool.

3 In a large mixing bowl combine cream cheese and the ½ cup sugar; beat with an electric mixer on medium speed until combined. Add eggs, beating just until combined. Beat in melted white chocolate just until combined. Spread over crust. Drizzle the reserved 2 tablespoons raspberry sauce over filling; carefully swirl with a knife to marble.

4 Bake in a 350° oven for 40 to 45 minutes or until center appears set when shaken. (Do not overbake.) Cool for 15 minutes in pan on a wire rack. Loosen crust from side of pan. Cool 30 minutes more; remove side of pan. Cool completely. Chill for at least 4 hours or up to 24 hours before slicing. Serve with remaining raspberry sauce.

Nutrition Facts per serving: 448 cal., 30 g total fat (18 g sat. fat), 130 mg chol., 321 mg sodium, 36 g carbo., 1 g fiber, 8 g pro.

Mesclun Salad with Roasted Pears

Roasting intensifies the flavor of the pears used in this elegant salad. Select Bosc pears for roasting—they hold their shape best.

Ingredients

2 pounds Bosc pears, peeled, cored, and sliced ¼ inch thick

1 tablespoon olive oil

½ teaspoon salt

¼ teaspoon freshly ground black pepper

¼ cup olive oil

2 tablespoons sherry vinegar or balsamic vinegar

2 teaspoons finely chopped shallots

1 teaspoon honey

2 5-ounce bags mesclun salad greens or spring salad mix (12 cups)

2 cups sliced fresh strawberries

3 ounces blue cheese, crumbled

¾ cup pecan halves, toasted (optional)

Prep: 20 minutes   **Roast:** 20 minutes   **Oven:** 425°F
Makes: 12 appetizer servings

1 Line a 15×10×1-inch baking pan with foil. Place pear slices in prepared pan. Drizzle with the 1 tablespoon oil. Sprinkle with ¼ teaspoon of the salt and ⅛ teaspoon of the pepper; toss to coat. Arrange slices in a single layer. Roast pear slices, uncovered, in a 425° oven for 20 to 25 minutes or until pears are golden and edges are crisp and brown, gently stirring and rearranging once. Watch closely the last few minutes of roasting to prevent burning. Cool in pan on a wire rack.

2 For dressing, in a screw-top jar combine the ¼ cup olive oil, the vinegar, shallots, honey, the remaining ¼ teaspoon salt and the remaining ⅛ teaspoon pepper. Cover; shake well.

3 Arrange greens, pear slices, strawberries, blue cheese, and, if desired, pecans on individual salad plates. Drizzle with the dressing.

Nutrition Facts per serving: 129 cal., 8 g total fat (2 g sat. fat), 5 mg chol., 198 mg sodium, 13 g carbo., 2 g fiber, 2 g pro.

Menu Options

Veal Roast with Herb Crust

Off-the-shelf herbs combine with dry bread crumbs to form a savory crust for this roast. The simple sour cream sauce makes a perfect partner.

Ingredients

1   3-pound boneless veal leg

    round roast

1   tablespoon olive oil

1   tablespoon Dijon-style mustard

1   tablespoon lemon juice

1   teaspoon dried basil, crushed

1   teaspoon dried thyme, crushed

½   teaspoon coarsely ground

    black pepper

2   tablespoons fine dry bread crumbs

1   cup beef broth

2   tablespoons all-purpose flour

¼   cup light dairy sour cream

Prep: 15 minutes   **Roast:** 2½ hours
Oven: 325°F   **Makes:** 10 to 12 main-dish servings

1 Place roast on a rack in a shallow roasting pan. In a small bowl stir together oil, mustard, lemon juice, basil, thyme, and pepper. Brush mixture over surface of roast. Sprinkle top of roast with bread crumbs.

2 Insert an oven-going meat thermometer in center of roast. Roast, uncovered, in a 325° oven for 2½ to 3 hours or until thermometer registers 160°F. (If crust becomes too dry, cover roast loosely with foil after 1½ to 2 hours of roasting.) Transfer roast to a warm serving platter; cover and keep warm.

3 For sauce, skim fat from pan drippings. In a small saucepan stir beef broth into flour; add pan drippings. Cook and stir until thickened and bubbly. Cook and stir for 1 minute more. Stir in the sour cream; heat through, but do not boil. Pass sauce with the roast.

Nutrition Facts per serving: 180 cal., 4 g total fat (1 g sat. fat), 108 mg chol., 217 mg sodium, 3 g carbo., 1 g fiber, 30 g pro.

Metric Information

The charts on this page provide a guide for converting measurements from the U.S. customary system, which is used throughout this book, to the metric system.

Product Differences

Most of the ingredients called for in the recipes in this book are available in most countries. However, some are known by different names. Here are some common American ingredients and their possible counterparts:

- Sugar (white) is granulated, fine granulated, or castor sugar.
- Powdered sugar is icing sugar.
- All-purpose flour is enriched, bleached or unbleached white household flour. When self-rising flour is used in place of all-purpose flour in a recipe that calls for leavening, omit the leavening agent (baking soda or baking powder) and salt.
- Light-colored corn syrup is golden syrup.
- Cornstarch is cornflour.
- Baking soda is bicarbonate of soda.
- Vanilla or vanilla extract is vanilla essence.
- Green, red, or yellow sweet peppers are capsicums or bell peppers.
- Golden raisins are sultanas.

Volume and Weight

The United States traditionally uses cup measures for liquid and solid ingredients. The chart below shows the approximate imperial and metric equivalents. If you are accustomed to weighing solid ingredients, the following approximate equivalents will be helpful.

- 1 cup butter, castor sugar, or rice = 8 ounces = ½ pound = 250 grams
- 1 cup flour = 4 ounces = ¼ pound = 125 grams
- 1 cup icing sugar = 5 ounces = 150 grams

Canadian and U.S. volume for a cup measure is 8 fluid ounces (237 ml), but the standard metric equivalent is 250 ml.

1 British imperial cup is 10 fluid ounces.

In Australia, 1 tablespoon equals 20 ml, and there are 4 teaspoons in the Australian tablespoon.

Spoon measures are used for smaller amounts of ingredients. Although the size of the tablespoon varies slightly in different countries, for practical purposes and for recipes in this book, a straight substitution is all that's necessary. Measurements made using cups or spoons always should be level unless stated otherwise.

Common Weight Range Replacements

Imperial / U.S.	Metric
½ ounce	15 g
1 ounce	25 g or 30 g
4 ounces (¼ pound)	115 g or 125 g
8 ounces (½ pound)	225 g or 250 g
16 ounces (1 pound)	450 g or 500 g
1¼ pounds	625 g
1½ pounds	750 g
2 pounds or 2¼ pounds	1,000 g or 1 Kg

Oven Temperature Equivalents

Fahrenheit Setting	Celsius Setting*	Gas Setting
300°F	150°C	Gas Mark 2 (very low)
325°F	160°C	Gas Mark 3 (low)
350°F	180°C	Gas Mark 4 (moderate)
375°F	190°C	Gas Mark 5 (moderate)
400°F	200°C	Gas Mark 6 (hot)
425°F	220°C	Gas Mark 7 (hot)
450°F	230°C	Gas Mark 8 (very hot)
475°F	240°C	Gas Mark 9 (very hot)
500°F	260°C	Gas Mark 10 (extremely hot)
Broil	Broil	Grill

*Electric and gas ovens may be calibrated using celsius. However, for an electric oven, increase celsius setting 10 to 20 degrees when cooking above 160°C. For convection or forced air ovens (gas or electric) lower the temperature setting 25°F/10°C when cooking at all heat levels.

Baking Pan Sizes

Imperial / U.S.	Metric
9×1½-inch round cake pan	22- or 23×4-cm (1.5 L)
9×1½-inch pie plate	22- or 23×4-cm (1 L)
8×8×2-inch square cake pan	20×5-cm (2 L)
9×9×2-inch square cake pan	22- or 23×4.5-cm (2.5 L)
11×7×1½-inch baking pan	28×17×4-cm (2 L)
2-quart rectangular baking pan	30×19×4.5-cm (3 L)
13×9×2-inch baking pan	34×22×4.5-cm (3.5 L)
15×10×1-inch jelly roll pan	40×25×2-cm
9×5×3-inch loaf pan	23×13×8-cm (2 L)
2-quart casserole	2 L

U.S. / Standard Metric Equivalents

⅛ teaspoon = 0.5 ml
¼ teaspoon = 1 ml
½ teaspoon = 2 ml
1 teaspoon = 5 ml
1 tablespoon = 15 ml
2 tablespoons = 25 ml
¼ cup = 2 fluid ounces = 50 ml
⅓ cup = 3 fluid ounces = 75 ml
½ cup = 4 fluid ounces = 125 ml
⅔ cup = 5 fluid ounces = 150 ml
¾ cup = 6 fluid ounces = 175 ml
1 cup = 8 fluid ounces = 250 ml
2 cups = 1 pint = 500 ml
1 quart = 1 litre